I0123418

The +Point. The Power of Positive Thinking for Everyone!

A 28-Day Self-Development Guide to Overcoming Negative Thinking, Anxiety, and Poor Motivation by Developing a Positive Mindset for a Happier, More Motivated You.

Jackson James

3 eye publishing

The +Point. The Power of Positive Thinking for Everyone!

Jackson James

Book Cover by Olina

1st edition 2023

Contents

The Big Hello

"The only thing standing between you and your goal is the story you keep telling yourself as to why you can't achieve it."[1]

Hello Everyone!

My name is Jackson James.

I will be your positivity guide and fellow traveling companion on this incredible journey to find your more positive self. Yes, and no matter what you think, you do have a more positive self and I promise that it is very much alive and kicking, although sometimes it's a little bit buried beneath the crap that life tends to throw our way.

During our journey together we will witness a place where the extraordinary becomes the exciting every day and the power of positivity is unshackled and unbound. A place where those who have not yet joined us for this epic road trip will stand on the sidewalk of life gobsmacked and amazed at how the transformed you will approach everything in life with undaunted optimism, drive, and determination to succeed. And until they join us on

---

1. Jordan Belfort, (2007), "The Wolf of Wall Street"

this quest they will never know what the hell happened to their friend, colleague, or loved one. Yes, it's going to be crazy, Yes, it's going to be wonderful, and Yes, it's going to change your life forever.

Here's a fact;

Your brain is big!

Now, I'm not just talking about physical dimensions here, although it has tripled in size throughout our evolution. No, I'm talking about its computable size. Stuffed inside your head are 86 Billion neurons packed tighter than sardines each connected to thousands of fellow neurons making for literally trillions of synaptic connections. It has a storage capacity of 2.5 petabytes of data. Nope, I didn't have a clue what a petabyte was either, but apparently, it is the equivalent of watching about three million hours of the morning show with Don, Poppy, and Kaitlin – not to be recommended! Not only is it big it's also mighty quick, pinging all that information around in there faster than a speeding helicopter. And did you know that your brain produces enough electricity to physically power a lightbulb? Now that's an idea!

Why am I telling you all this?

Well, it's to make you aware of just how amazingly privileged we all are as a species to be carrying around in our heads over a hundred thousand Macbook Pros and not fall over. Therefore it seems an awful shame that once bestowed with such an amazing technological marvel we allow it to fall into the realms of negativity and moan about our latte not being hot enough, or the rain being too wet or the grass being the wrong shade of green. Imagine a world in which we didn't mind if the latte we held didn't have our name spelled correctly on the side or if the grass had not been mowed that week, and we concentrated our energies on the more positive aspects of our lives, overcoming negativity in a single 'Super-sized' bound. Think of the possibilities that would exist, at home, at work, and at play. Think of a world where the human mind was attuned to making positive decisions, overcoming adversity, and making the world a better place without the need for taxes or speeding tickets. Well, my fellow seekers of positive thinking that is the journey that we are about to embark upon. Feel the fear Tax Inspectors and do it anyway.

Now before we start our journey I should properly introduce myself as no one likes to travel with strangers, do they?

I am Jackson James and yes my name does sound like I'm back-to-front. Thank you, Mom and Dad. They named my sister Josephine. I think I would have preferred that. She never seemed to complain.

I was born and raised in London. That's London England and not London Island, London Ontario, London Arkansas or any of the other twenty-six pretend Londons out there just to confuse matters. None of which have our red buses, black taxis, and as many particulates in their atmosphere to chew upon.

I was educated to a highly acceptable standard in Cambridge to the delight of my father and then decided to explore the world rather than take up a proper job, much to his disgust. I ventured around the globe spending time in Europe before we disowned them, Asia before we distrusted them, and America before we disapproved of the leadership. Over the years I have put my deep knowledge of Psychology and Human Interaction to good work having been employed by some of the largest corporations seeking to get more from their often somewhat disenfranchised workers by shaping their efforts to best fit the business. This led me into the wondrous field of 'Positive Psychology' which I put to even greater use by shaping these businesses around their employees. I am now residing in the Bay Area of San Francisco enjoying the cafes, wine bars, and lattes with my name spelled back to front.

Why is this important? Well, I have been reliably informed by my agent that this getting-to-know-each-other phase of the book is rather important, where we bond and you guys are left with absolute certainty that I'm the guy you should be listening to when it comes to whatever is printed on the front cover, in this case, **Positive Thinking**. Now to make this more of a Unibond moment I can also tell you that what I am proposing in this book is proven. It works. 100 % Fact! I have been using it for many years, in many places around the planet, and encouraging others to do the same for equally as many years and I thank my lucky stars that no one else has had the inclination to write it all down and publish it before me. The other important fact is that this book is not some regurgitated ideas written with different words and misspellings. What lies ahead of us is truly new and innovative. A specific combination of certain exercises and knowledge transfers that all combine to move your internal barometer from chilly negativity to warm and sunny positivity just by changing the way we think about stuff.

Another important thing to cover is who this book is written for. Now conventional wisdom dictates that when writing a book you should first seek out a specific niche such as Business owners in High Heels and target that group so that your book resonates and magically jumps up the best-seller chart for that particular niche of Business owners with overly tight-fitting footwear. Now to my agent's annoyance, with the distinct possibility of her wagging a bony finger in my direction later and saying "I told you so", I have chosen to totally disregard this advice. Sorry conventional wisdom! Maybe next time.

This book is focused specifically on everyone. I know that sounds like a bit of a contradiction but go with me on this. It's not just for business, although it contains lots of business scenarios. It's not just for use in your private life, although it has a lot of those examples crammed in too. It's a book designed for every occasion, for everyone, young, old, alive or dead. There is no reason why you can't use any of the strategies that I have lovingly crafted here at any point in your life or afterlife. And the good news is that by implementing this system of strategies you will be empowered to change your entire existence in the most positive ways possible (no pun intended). This book is for the 'many people' who want to refocus their brains to reflect the power of positive thinking for their lifelong success.

There's one other thing to mention before we get started. I am a lover of good grammar. I do respect it and a book with correct punctuation and grammar is a joy to read. This is not one of those books. Sorry for you competing grammar lovers out there. I have ignored some of the stricture and structure that come with writing a correctly edited and well-grammared book simply because we are going to have a conversation and I simply don't talk like that. I tend to start sentences with And for instance and a whole load of Buts. I did try to follow the rules but I really don't think that you will likely talk that way either, so for all grammar aficionados, please don't judge me.

Now within my opening introduction, I intentionally neglected to mention any of the hard times that I have encountered. You know, those tough moments along life's journey where you end up traveling down a road that leads to pretty dark places. And I'm not just talking about Dagenham here. I'm talking downright depressing times. Times that you would like to forget but frustratingly keep on popping back up into your memory just after an episode of Plane Crash Investigates. However, what has always seen me through those bad times is…… people. I bet you thought I was going to say positive thinking :) Well maybe a close second but like everything in life as far as I have found in my forty-two rotations around the sun, people make the real difference. That's you and I and everyone who is on this journey with us and beyond.

People make the difference, but rarely the negative ones, or if they do it's for all the wrong reasons. Think of Traffic Wardens. Consider the last time you reached out to someone when you really needed help. I mean a situation where you had little choice but to find an ally and seek their support. Did you reach out to someone who actually helped? Did that someone have a positive or negative disposition? I bet they were of the former. You know the ones I mean. The ones that don't let the negativity of life, get in the way. The men and women of this planet who carry around with them a distinct magical aura that silently whispers to those that know them well, 'I have your back', 'You can count on me'. Those are the people I mean and these are the people we shall be.

The Call for Transformation

Have you ever found yourself ensnared in the relentless web of negativity, where the world seems shrouded in darkness, and hope feels like a long-lost memory? Have you ever yearned for a seed of hope, a shred of positivity, something however small to keep you going? Yep, I've been there; calling in at destination deep depression – lost amidst the shadows of pessimism, ensnared in a whirlwind of deepest self-doubt, and hungering for just a mere glimmer of light amid the gloom of utter despair.

Perhaps, you've tasted the bitterness of overwhelm, the disillusionment of dreams deferred, and the labyrinthine existence of a life mired in the stickiness of negativity. Or possibly worse still, you've been merely existing, a passive spectator on the sidewalk of life, where joy is but a faint echo and dreams are mere fragments of forgotten aspirations. It sounds totally shitty because it really, truly is. Those of us who have suffered, or are suffering, you know just how bad it can really get.

But here's the thing: no matter where you're coming from, no matter how deep the abyss may seem at the time, there is always a path out of the darkness. A path illuminated by positivity where we can all bask in the warmth of the knowledge that we can make a difference, we can get through it and we can be successful! The power of positive thinking is one of the greatest powers on this planet and we are on a whistle-stop tour to discover how to claim it for ourselves.

In the chapters that follow, we'll embark on a transformative journey, one that will guide you from despair to hope, from negativity to positivity, and from mere existence to a life filled with joy, purpose, and resilience. Together, we'll uncover the extraordinary power of positive thinking, and in just 28 days, you'll witness a far brighter, more positive you.

I shall be your mentor and fellow passenger, if you will have me, on this express train of self-discovery and personal trans-formation. Together, we shall rewrite the script of your life, and illuminate the path to positivity. But make no mistake; this is no ordinary self-help book. It's your invitation to a life filled with unwavering optimism, boundless resilience, and limitless possi-bilities.

Embrace "The +Point Process"

At the core of our journey lies an innovation that I hold close to my heart – "**The +Point Process.**" It's not just a philosophy; it's a life-altering system, a compass to navigate the pathways of your mind and the challenges of existence. The +Point is about tapping into the infinite reservoirs of positivity, rewiring your thought patterns, and navigating life's twists and turns with unwavering courage, unyielding resilience, and unshakable optimism, oh, and we will have a little bit of fun along the way. In short, it's a map, a glorious full-color treasure map guiding you through the treacherous terrain of negativity toward the boundless riches of positivity.

This innovative process will help you unearth your inner strengths, discover the hidden gems of your potential, and em-power you to transcend the limitations that have held you back for so long. It will challenge your existing beliefs, broaden your horizons, and infuse your life with newfound purpose and vitality. Each day of our 28-day expedition will unveil a new facet of The +Point Process, equipping you with the right tools, strategies, and mindset needed to forge a brighter more successful future.

Excited? I am!

***

All aboard!

So, the whistle has been blown, the graffiti-covered doors are closing tight and the engine is whirring into life. The train is about to leave the station, are you all aboard?

If you are then your golden Willy Wonka railroad ticket will take you to where the shadows of despair have been cast asunder by the radiant glow of positivity. A place where your spirit will be set free and you will rise above the negativity that engulfs our world. By unlocking the secrets to transforming our lives we will rekindle the flames of desire, drive, determination, and unbridled success! Our journey is not just about personal growth; it is a revolution! – a call to arms to fight for your right to the power of positive thinking.

Join me, and together, we shall set the world aglow with the brilliance of our positivity!

***

Chapter One

The Power of Positive Thinking

"Happiness can be found even in the darkest of times if one only remembers to turn on the light."[1]

⸎

Welcome to the inaugural chapter of our exploration of the marvels of positive thinking and what lies behind the sciencey bits.

The Psychological Marvel of Positivity

Our journey together commences with an exploration of the human psyche. The human mind is a truly wonderful piece of

---

1.

    J.K. Rowling, (1999), "Harry Potter and the Prisoner of Azkaban" engineering, with unlimited storage capacity, the ability to ping information all about faster than a Lamborgini on full throttle, and capable of literally powering a lightbulb, for all those...light-bulb moments. Your brain is incredibly adaptable too and has what is called Neuroplasticity, which in layman's terms means that it can rewire itself like having an inbuilt IT helpdesk that speaks your language. Neat! This means it can learn, recover from injury, and adapt to new experiences and situations as it is exposed to them. It can also conjure remarkable transformations when engaged in the alchemy of positive thinking. Because at its core, positive thinking is a catalyst for a profound shift in our mind's mental landscape. It's like prizing opening the windows of a stuffy room to let the smell of fish and chips waft in.

Now, let's get down to the nitty-gritty of psychology. Positive thinking isn't just a warm fuzzy feeling after a Scotch and American, or that warm glow after amazing sex, although that's probably getting a little closer. Neither is it a fleeting mood swing like 'Hey today I will be less grumpy', no it's an entire outlook on life that can dramatically reshape your reality. People in long white coats have been researching this stuff for years and after much scribbling and debate, possibly at the same time, agreed that positive thoughts, possibly about great sex, encourage your brain to release a cascade of feel-good neurotransmitters, such as dopamine and serotonin. This neurochemical concoction is akin to the sparks that ignite a fireworks display inside our brains, creating an atmosphere of happiness and reduced stress, with absolutely no smoke.

So here's a scenario for you; You wake at 6 a.m. to the Power Rangers theme tune that mysteriously uploaded itself to your mobile phone several days ago and for some inexplicable reason, known only by the phone's manufacturers, refuses to budge from the alarm setting. Having yet to work out the complexities of the snooze function you prod and swipe randomly until "Go Go Power Rangers, Mighty Morphin' Power Rangers " suddenly relents. You are now wide awake and another work day beckons. Laying back down in the refreshing silence you could succumb to the gravitational pull of pessimism or you could choose a different direction from your last five years and embrace positive thinking about your day ahead. Immediately your brain will respond in kind and possibly with some surprise, by rewarding you with a giant burst of dopamine, making you immediately feel more energetic, motivated, and ready to tackle the challenges of the day. This isn't mere wishful thinking; it's the neural science of positivity all at work in your bed!

<hr />

Neuroplasticity: The Brain's Remarkable Adaptability

So I mentioned Neuroplasticity and the fact that our brains are not static entities but dynamic and super-adaptable creations. Neuroplasticity is like the master architect behind the scenes, re-arranging the neural furniture to accommodate all our thoughts and experiences. Think of it like a giant ball of playdough. If that helps.

When we practice positive thinking consistently, we're essentially forging new neural pathways in our brains. Each time we make a conscious choice to think positively, we strengthen these pathways and build new ones, making it easier for us to lean into optimism and resilience. In essence, positive thinking isn't just a fleeting emotion; it's a cognitive skill that we can hone and cultivate over time. Once given the knowledge and skills to apply it anyone and everyone can make it part of how they think and how they act. And that means you.

The Ripple Effect

Now, let's venture beyond the confines of our own individual minds and explore the social dimensions that positive thinking has. Positivity has a ripple effect that extends far beyond our personal experiences. It's like tossing a pebble into a pond and watching the ripples spread, affecting everyone in their wake.

This can make an awful lot of difference in any scenario. Say you have made it out of bed and reached the office. You find that your team is facing a particularly stressful project with G-string tight deadlines. Instead of succumbing to negativity and complaining all about it, you consciously choose to maintain a positive attitude seeking solutions and opportunities to move forward at pace. Your optimism becomes contagious, influencing your colleagues to approach the project with greater enthusiasm and a can-do spirit. The workplace instantly transforms into a more harmonious and productive environment for all, even those with tight underwear.

The Significance of Sustaining Positivity

But why should we bother with all this positive thinking business? Can't we just go about our daily lives without giving it much thought? Well, here's the crux of the matter: positivity is more than a pleasant state of mind; it's your secret weapon for navigating the often turbulent waters of life day in, and day out.

When we cultivate a positive mindset, we become like ships equipped with sturdy anchors in the face of storms. We sail through life's challenges with greater ease, bounce back from setbacks with resilience, and remain undeterred by stress, or high seas. Don't think of Positivity as a nice to have or a luxury item. Think of it as a key driver of your overall well-being and quality of life irrespective of where you are, at work, at home, or down the pub.

Here's a scenario you may recognize, and one that I relate to; where everything seems to be falling apart. Your career is hanging by a thread, your relationships are fraying, and self-doubt is tying you up in knots. It's at moments like these, when you have run out of rope analogies, that positive thinking becomes your steadfast ally. It reminds you that all challenges are opportunities in disguise and that you possess the inner strength to conquer them. This change in mindset at the right crucial moment can make the difference between succumbing to failure or grasping hold of success with both hands.

A colleague of mine once said, " Jackson, you can fall in a bucket of shit and still come up smelling of roses". Now I don't think that they were being particularly kind at the time but it does go to show you that those of us with a positive thinking mindset smell a whole lot better than those without.

So, the takeaway is that all this Positive Thinking is not some mumbo jumbo that guys wanting to sell a few million books on the subject makeup, it really does make a whole lot of sense and is scientifically proven. The potential to transform your life by acquiring the skill of positive thinking truly exists and lucky for you I have written the whole lot down in this easy-to-follow book.

By delving deep into the psychology and neuroscience of positive thinking, you're arming yourself with the knowledge required to rewrite your life's narrative. It's not just about feeling good; it's about thriving, regardless of the storms that may come your way.

Over next chapters, we will dive deeper into 'The +Point Process', our guiding star in the universe of positivity. Until then, keep those positive thoughts flowing, because the best of you is yet to come!

Chapter Two

The +Point Process to Positive Thinking

"Keep your face always toward the sunshine—and shadows will fall behind you."[1]

Ladies and gentlemen welcome to a chapter that promises to unveil a transformative approach to positive thinking—**The +Point Process**. Here we'll explore the revolutionary nature of this innovative system, its departure from conventional positive thinking methods, and its impressive track record in delivering lasting change.

1.

Walt Whitman,(1855), "Leaves of Grass"

The Grand Unveiling

You're at a first-night showing, all dressed up in your finest tux. The lights dim, you adjust your dickie, and the curtains to the grand stage pull majestically aside. Dadah.. a shimmering light shines down from the heavens its intense beam picking out a startling revelation within the inky darkness. The crowd gasps as they gain a full appreciation of the miracle that stands resolutely before them. Success! Yes success in their lives for all time, success at work, success in relationships, success in getting the duvet inside its cover, well maybe that's outside the realms of possibility. But success certainly is within your grasp. And it all rests upon something truly, amazingly, uniquely, extraordinary. I like to call it the +Point for reasons that I will go through later on. The +Point is a process dedicated to creating, enhancing, and reinforcing positive thinking as a repeatable routine in our daily lives. No self-help gimmick here. No one-size-fits-all lame solutions that you will forget the instant that the cover closes. This is a comprehensive, evidence-based approach that redefines how we understand and apply positive thinking throughout our lives. Oh, and it works. Fact!

Traditional Approaches

Before we dive headlong into the intricacies of The +Point Process, let's contrast it with conventional positive thinking approaches, which are often characterized by somewhat surface-level practices that provide temporary relief but rarely result in real lasting change.

Positive Affirmations:

Traditional positive thinking frequently revolves around the use of positive affirmations—short, optimistic statements that individuals repeat to themselves regularly. For example, someone might say, "I am confident and successful" or "I am surrounded by abundance." While these affirmations can momentarily boost one's mood and self-esteem, they often don't work in a McDonald's drive-thru. They lack the depth and the scientific grounding needed for sustainable change to really take place. Like a twig bridge, they may offer some support, but they are inherently fragile and don't address the root causes of negativity.

Visualization Exercises:

Another common practice involves visualizing desired outcomes. People are encouraged to vividly imagine achieving their goals, believing that this mental rehearsal will manifest their lifelong aspirations. While visualization can be a powerful tool for motivation, it often lacks the comprehensive framework needed for any long-term transformation. It's like attempting to cross the river with a makeshift raft—it might work for a short distance, but it's not a sustainable solution and your feet get wet.

Forced Positivity:

Some individuals try to suppress negative thoughts and emotions, believing that this will lead to a more positive mindset. However, this "fake it till you make it" approach can be emotionally exhausting and ultimately ineffective. It's as if lying to yourself continually will make it all better somehow. "I am not an author", "I am not an author"... damn it. Nope, don't work. Using my bridge analogy it's akin to constructing a rickety bridge from any available materials without considering the engineering principles—it might hold for a moment, but it's not a reliable path.

Superficial Optimism:

Traditional methods may also promote superficial optimism, encouraging people to put on a happy face even when facing adversity. While maintaining a positive demeanor can be valuable in certain situations, it doesn't address the underlying causes of negativity. It's like putting a new paint job on an old dilapidated bridge made of sticks and stuff.. you're getting my drift. It may look better until the paint wears thin but the structural issues remain the same.

Lack of Scientific Foundation:

Perhaps the most significant difference between these traditional approaches and The +Point Process is the scientific foundation. Traditional methods often lack empirical evidence and psychological insights, making them far less reliable for achieving lasting change. In contrast, The +Point Process is deeply rooted in scientific research, providing a super solid, evidence-based bridge to lasting positivity.

So what I am saying is that you can consider The +Point Process as your sturdy, well-made, and nicely painted bridge, meticulously engineered to carry you across the river with confidence and grace. It's engineered in science, and its effectiveness extends far beyond the banks of fleeting feel-good moments. It's not just a tool for you professionals out there, or to support you in your private life, it is a system to support everyone, everywhere and in everything. With The +Point Process, you're not just crossing the river; you're embarking on a transformative journey towards a brighter, more positive future full of lasting success!

Negativity

I think it wise at this stage to introduce our arch nemesis negativity. Now this insidious creature creeps and sulks about waiting for the exact moments when things don't turn out well. You know the ones I mean, The car doesn't start, your relationship hits an icy patch, the dog wee's on your shoes. At that 'point,' negativity will jump out and dive down your ear to ravage your brain. It loves stressors like worry, anxiety, self-doubt, and fear. They are its proverbial Sunday roast with all the trimmings and some nice thick Bistro gravy on the side, to feed upon. Negativity likes to consume and it has a rather ravenous appetite. The thing with negativity is that it is habit-forming too. Once it gets inside your mind you start to see more and more situations as negative experiences.

Let's go back to the car scenario. Negativity will tell you that your beloved 2019 Audi R8 V10+ in Suzuka grey and matching 20" alloys is a piece of crap. It hasn't started twice now and the engine must be on its way out even though it's still looking pretty lovely through the rear glass screen. Negativity will tell you that the depreciation alone would have paid for that Kia Picanto and that came with a full seven-year warranty that you should have gotten yourself in the first place. Think of the savings you could have made. You were an absolute idiot for buying such an expensive show car. And hey it's broken already and I bet it will cost an arm and a leg to fix and then you won't be able to sell it to anyone. See negativity doesn't like anyone to succeed or enjoy happiness, or even a great-sounding V10.

And that relationship, well he's been an arsehole for as long as you can remember but he's the best you could get. He's probably going to dump you and then your whole life will just fall apart. No one else will ever love you. Yep, I've heard those voices too, eroding self-confidence, sowing seeds of doubt, and creating fear and anxiety to feed yet more fear and anxiety. And worse of all is that if you ever meet a similar situation again guess what... yep you guessed it, you automatically return to all the bad feelings that flew through your head faster than that speeding Lamborgini.

Yes, I'm painting a dark, morose picture here I know, but if you are ever caught in negativities grip it can seriously hold you back. Think for a moment about certain work situations. How many times has negativity told you that you can't do something? "Don't go for that promotion. You will never get it and you'll only feel terrible afterward and then everyone will get to know what an utter failure you really are". Just think of how many times this negative self-talk has stopped you from trying something new and succeeding at it. So yeah, Negativity is pretty dark and pretty evil and can be found sneaking about almost anywhere. But don't fear for the force is strong with us and we have the power to use our Jedi mind tricks to defeat negativity once and for all and I am going to show you just how. Come my padawan let's now explore real evidence-based positivity.

Evidence-Based Foundation

The +Point Process isn't a collection of vague platitudes or motivational quotes; it's an evidence-based powerhouse of positivity firmly grounded in scientific research. Multiple studies have highlighted the profound impact of increased levels of positive thinking on both mental and physical well-being. Let's spend a moment exploring these compelling scientific foundations that prove that this system isn't your everyday self-help spiel, rather it forms a transformational catalyst for your holistic success.

Enhanced Immunity:

Scientific research has consistently demonstrated that maintaining a positive mindset can have a significant impact on the immune system. When you engage in positive thinking it sets off a chain reaction, summoning immune-boosting proteins such as interleukins and interferons, the commandos of your immune system. These protein protectors enhance your immunity helping to not only ward off common illnesses like colds and flu but also play a role in combating more serious conditions like cancer.

Stress Reduction:

Chronic stress is known to have serious detrimental effects on both our mental and physical health. Positive thinking can act as a powerful buffer against such stress. Studies have shown that if you practice positive thinking techniques you will experience reduced levels of cortisol, the stress hormone, leading to diminished stress-related health issues such as hypertension, anxiety disorders, and depression.

Improved Overall Health:

The mind-body connection is a well-established concept in medical research. Positive thinking not only affects mental health but also has cascading effects on your physical health. If you equip yourself with a strong positive outlook you are far more likely to engage in health-promoting behaviors like regular exercise, balanced nutrition, and sound sleep. This holistic approach, in turn, contributes to your improved overall health and an extended vibrant life.

Pain Management:

Positivity has been shown to influence the perception and management of pain. Studies show that if you foster a positive mindset you will tend to have higher pain tolerances and better pain management strategies. This can be particularly valuable for those dealing with chronic pain conditions.

By incorporating these scientific findings into positive thinking, The +Point Process provides a well-researched and systematic framework for achieving personal transformations. It doesn't rely on wishful thinking but on proven methods whose results are rooted in empirical evidence.

So think of Positive Thinking as your magical superfood. You will feel better, live longer, remain calmer, and be happier even when those around you are losing their heads.

Chapter Three

The +Point Overview

"The first step toward change is awareness. The second step is acceptance." [1]

We have run through traditional methods of instilling positive thinking and their individual lack of long-term success. We have had a look into the inner workings of that nasty little creature called negativity and its impact on our ball of playdough. And we have taken a look at evidence-based foundations to ensure that what we put in place really does work. Now, let's grab an overview of The +Point Process by breaking down the essential principles encapsulated in the "R.E.S.E.T." framework. Yes, everyone loves a good acronym, don't they.

The +Point Process Building Blocks

The R.E.S.E.T Framework is the key, fundamental building block that forms the backbone of The +Point Process. Like a great transformation plan, these building blocks will transport you through the phases of awareness, acceptance, adoption, and advocacy in a nice linear fashion like breakfast, lunch, and dinner, with a nice little dessert thrown in for good measure.

Now, let's take our first peek under the hood of the R.E.S.E.T. framework and get ourselves familiar with its five key principles that we will use later during our journey.

Principle #1: Recognize:

This is the starting point of your journey. It all starts with recognition. It's like exploring uncharted territory, and then someone presents you with Google Maps. Before setting out in a new direction you need to be aware of where you are coming from like learning the lay of the land. In this principle phase of the process, we are talking about recognizing the terrain of your own thoughts – those patterns that grab you by the hand and lead you down the road to either positive or negative destinations.

Principle #2: Explore:

So here we are, like modern-day explorers in the realm of self-awareness. This is where we roll up our sleeves and delve deep into the inner workings of our psyche. Think of it as donning a miner's helmet and descending into the intricate caves and caverns of your consciousness. Here, you'll uncover hidden treasures: the beliefs, past experiences, and detailed thought processes that you accept to govern how you react in certain situations. It's like spelunking into your own brain, where you uncover hidden potential whilst navigating through the labyrinth of your thoughts.

Principle #3: Shift:

Now, we are on a roll and turning the tide in the battle with negativity. Shifting from a negative to a positive mindset is a pivotal aspect of The +Point Process. It's not about denying the existence of obstacles but adjusting your perspective to them at the point when they arise. It's like fine-tuning your lens or finding the perfect pair of glasses that allow you to focus on the opportunities amid all of the challenges. As you master this skill, you'll find yourself adopting a new approach by charting a course through life's turbulent waters with renewed vigor, determination, and success.

Principle #4: Embrace:

Once you've embarked on this transformative journey, it's time to adopt positivity as your constant companion. Yep, I'm talking about getting a habit, a great habit. Think of embracing positivity like nurturing a seedling into a flourishing plant. You water it with gratitude and provide sunlight through affirmations, aiding its growth. It's not about pretending that negativity doesn't exist; it's about letting positivity take root in your daily routine. Just as a gardener tends to their plants each day, your daily practices will contribute to the blossoming of optimism within you.

Principle #5: Transform:

Transform is the equivalent of reaching the summit of our journey! Through unwavering dedication and the application of The +Point principles, you'll undergo a profound metamorphosis. This transformation isn't a magic trick; it's the result of consistent effort and dedication, following the system step by step to achieve your goals. But be warned people will start to look at you differently. They will stand back and stare, amazed at your sudden drive, enthusiasm, and general pizzazz, like blinded rabbits in the headlights of success. The change will be spectacular and remarkable and then you will feel obliged to advocate this change to others by coming back and giving my book a five-star rating on Amazon. This will help the other millions of people out there know where to go to fight the evil that is negativity and vastly improve their success quotient.

This is just a taster of what's to come when we traverse the full in-depth detail of the R.E.S.E.T. framework.

Evidence of Effectiveness

You might now be wondering, "Do these principles and this evidence-based system work?" OK, So you are already sold on the far-reaching holistic benefits of positive thinking and cultivating a positive attitude, but will what you are reading actually help to make you more positive?

Well, the answer my friends is a resounding yes. The +Point Process isn't based on mere theories; it's founded on real-world results and true success stories. Successes that I have witnessed play out with all those that I have taught to use this process. Many individuals, from various walks of life, have applied The +Point Process and witnessed truly remarkable transformations. These aren't just anecdotal tales of fleeting positivity but compelling accounts of enduring change. From overcoming adversity to achieving personal goals and ultimate success, the effectiveness of this system speaks volumes. Here are some studies on a number of the +Point process elements to help make that point clear:

The Impact of Positive Psychology:

There have been numerous studies in the field of positive psychology that have shown that cultivating a positive mindset can lead to increased overall well-being, lower levels of depression, and improved life satisfaction. Leading researchers and pioneers in the world of Positive Psychology like Martin Seligman, Ph.D. and Barbara Fredrickson, Ph.D. have contributed heavily to this body of work.

The Role of Gratitude:

In-depth research on the role of gratitude in our lives, such as the studies conducted by Robert Emmons, Ph.D. and Michael McCullough Ph.D. have demonstrated that consciously practicing gratitude can lead to increased positive emotions, better health, and stronger relationships overall.

Mindfulness and Stress Reduction:

Studies on mindfulness-based practices, including meditation and mindfulness-based stress reduction (MBSR), have shown their effectiveness in reducing stress, and anxiety and promoting well-being. Researchers like Jon Kabat-Zinn Ph.D. have been pioneers in this field for many years.

Neuroplasticity: Neuroscientific research has revealed that the brain is capable of rewiring itself. Norman Doidge MD, Ph.D. in his book "The Brain That Changes Itself," covers how changes in thought patterns and behaviors can lead to actual changes in brain structure and function.

Social Support and Positive Influence: Research by social psychologists like Nicholas Christakis, MD, Ph.D. MPH and James Fowler Ph.D. has highlighted the power of social networks and the influence of positive and negative emotions within these networks. Surrounding oneself with positive individuals can have a profound impact on your personal positivity.

These are just some of the studies that provide a solid scientific foundation for the concepts and practices related to the +Point principles of positive thinking. The principles leverage these insights to guide individuals in rewiring their thought patterns, enhancing their emotional well-being, and ultimately leading to a healthier, more fulfilling, and longer life.

When we talk about The +Point Process principles, we're not just discussing abstract concepts; we're delving into scientifically validated approaches that will empower you to harness the tangible benefits of positive thinking for your entire life.

In the following chapters, we'll delve even deeper into how The +Point Process can be practically applied in your life. Get ready to discover the concrete steps and strategies that will lead you toward lasting positive change.

Chapter Four

The RESET Framework

"I am not afraid of storms, for I am learning how to sail my ship" [1]

Alright, buckle up, because we're about to take a voyage deep into The +Point Process one principle at a time. No more skimming the surface; we're going to explore the inner workings like a curious kid taking apart their Christmas present to see how it works. So, grab a notepad (or open your Positivity journal), because you'll want to remember all this.

---

1. Louisa May Alcott, (1868), "Little Women"

The R.E.S.E.T. Framework: A Five-Step Process

The +Point Process is engineered across five key principles. These principles allow you to identify the likely moments of negativity, understand why those moments occur, create defenses against such occurrences, identify methods to utilize positivity appropriately, and then make your responses habit-forming. It really is a straightforward step-by-step process that anyone can follow and achieve remarkable results with.

The reason why I have named it The +Point Process is so that it clearly states what it does on the side of the tin. It's about using each of these five principles at the '*point*' of thought creation. Let's face it there is no use walking around all day smiling like a Cheshire cat at things and sending out positive vibes in all directions. One, it's way too tiring, and two you will achieve very little apart from looking ever so slightly strange to everyone you meet.

Timing, as always, is everything. Like a good tune, get the melody and the chorus timed just right and you'll have a hit. The beauty with The +Point Process, if you use it correctly, is that you will have hit after hit after hit without wasting time on the things that really don't matter. It's your laser-guided missile for cutting through the noise of life and getting on with the success that you deserve, all packaged in one little book. Moreover, It's about not accepting the norms of our world as it exists today and choosing the precise point in time to be positive to fulfill your goals. So the '+ 'is for positive thinking and taking action and the 'point', represents the precise moment in time to use each of the five principles. OK, you can see that I'm no rocket scientist when it comes to naming things.

So let us walk through each one of the five stages or principles of the system in detail over the following Chapters starting with R for Recognition and identify what each one deals with, how each works, and what you need to do to maximize your level of success.

Chapter Five

Principle #1: Recognize

"The better you know yourself, the better your relationship with the rest of the world." [1]

Recognize: The Thought Detective

Welcome to the first core principle and the utterly thrilling world of '**Recognize,**' where you become the star detective of your very own thought universe. Who doesn't like a bit of role-play! This principle is all about self-discovery and insight. Imagine it as your trusty magnifying glass, and you, the keen detective, are about to

---

1. Toni Collette (n.d.) As cited in James Jackson (2023) The +Point. The Power of Positive Thinking for Everyone!

uncover the mysteries of your own mind. Creepy right? But also really exciting at the same time.

Let's kick off with some exercises that you will need to undertake to get this principle well and truly under your belt.

Exercise 1: The Daily Thought Journal

Your journey as a thought detective begins with the Daily Thought Journal. This is your investigator's notebook, where you'll jot down your thoughts and feelings throughout the day. Here's how it works:

The Play-by-Play:

As you go about your day, attune yourself to notice when there is a noticeable shift in your mood whether that's positive or negative. Your mood change may be triggered by a person, a situation, or even by a passing thought.

Now up until this moment, you have probably become fairly desensitized to these inner changes, especially in the daily hustle and bustle of life. I mean who takes the time to think about why they feel a certain way and when that certain way started to happen? Well, this is where you will begin to do exactly that and learn all about yourself at the same time. This is the most important principle so don't think you can skip it. If you are serious about changing your entire life then you need to put in the work. No pain, no gain, you know how it goes. You will need to be on the lookout for the tail-tail signs of your mood changes. Don't worry if you miss a few to start with but try to pause each time you notice a change within yourself and scribble it down in your journal as soon as you can.

The Whodunit:

Whenever you record a thought or feeling, ask yourself, "What triggered this? Why did I react this way?" Dive deeper into the circumstances surrounding your mood shift and make a note next to it under a separate column headed triggers. Were you feeling threatened or perhaps you didn't have all the facts to hand? Maybe your memory wasn't playing ball or you had previously had a good or bad experience doing the same thing. Consider your responses in detail to certain situations; for example, if someone disagrees with your perspective on things, or if you don't get your own way. These situations and others will provide you with a wealth of knowledge and self-understanding. It's important that you take a moment to reflect and truthfully explore each occurrence as it happens. Using introspection to understand your responses to situations like these will begin the process of understanding yourself and making the changes to your mindset required for positive success.

The Plot Thickens:

I want you to make this an ongoing habit. Always have your journal to hand and note down your mood changes. I suggest that each week you take time to review that week's entries. Over time, you'll start to notice certain reoccurring patterns or themes. Perhaps every Monday morning, you feel a sense of dread. Or your stress levels go through the roof each time you need to present something important to your boss. Maybe every time you see a certain friend, you're filled with joy, or each time you take a walk in the park you feel relaxed and at one with nature. These patterns are precious clues that you need to gather and then unravel to get to the bottom of your thought mysteries.

Understanding Dawns:

After two or three weeks of diligent journaling, you will have gathered a collection of insights into your thought patterns and triggers. You may discover recurring themes, situations that consistently impact your mood in the same way, or even hidden beliefs that influence your reactions. The Daily Thought Journal serves as your first foundational step toward self-awareness. By recognizing and documenting your thoughts and triggers, you'll gain a deeper understanding of your inner workings. This exercise alone can lead to reduced anxiety, better stress management, and improved emotional regulation.

Exercise #2: Dialogue Diary

In this unique exercise, we will delve into the fascinating realm of your inner dialogue, uncovering the stories that you tell yourself. Think of it as eavesdropping on your mind's secret conversations:

Create Your Dialogue Diary:

Dedicate a section in your journal to this exercise. I would suggest creating a third column headed 'Dialogue' to go next to your columns headed 'Moods' and "Triggers". That way as you note the changes in your mood throughout your day you can add dialogue detail next to it which I will go through in a moment. If time is tight this is something that you should make a mental note of and come back to as soon as you can. But be aware, the longer you leave to get it down on paper the less you will remember and the more inaccurate it will be.

The Inner Observer:

The voices, the voices! Yes, there are voices in your head. Don't worry this is perfectly natural as you internally verbalize your thoughts. Throughout your day, pay close attention to these conversations happening inside your skull. Are you often critical of yourself? Do you tend to doubt your abilities? Do you dismiss others? Alternatively, do you relish certain experiences or activities or look forward to meeting certain individuals? Write down these inner dialogues as they occur with any associated mood changes.

Dialogue Analysis:

Each week review your recorded inner dialogues and categorize them. Are they self-critical, self-doubting, or self-encouraging? Identify recurring themes and the triggers that initiate these conversations. Perhaps you may start a separate list for the 'Recurring favorites', creating a top ten for your recurring dialogue themes.

Challenge and Reframe:

Now here comes the next important bit. For every self-critical or self-doubting dialogue you've documented, challenge its validity. Ask yourself if there's evidence to the contrary. Practice reframing these dialogues with more positive and empowering alternatives. For the presentation example; how did it go with your boss? Did he criticize the hell out of your pitch or did he respond positively to it? How did your interaction go during the rest of the meeting? Note down your reframed alternative in a fourth column next to the recorded dialogue.

Often allowing your mind to simply accept negative self-dialogue will make it a self-sustaining prophecy. What I mean by that is if we keep telling ourselves that we can't do something, then more often than not we will fail at it or most likely be too afraid to even try. As I said negativity can be a terrible creature, infesting our minds with bad thoughts and self-doubt. But don't think that you are alone in this, oh no you can bet your bottom dollar that most of the people that you meet are suffering from the same debilitating infestation. The great news is that you are being given the cure.

The Output:

Your Dialogue Diary will reveal the stories that your mind constructs. You'll have a record of your inner dialogues, their triggers, and your attempts to reframe them. By unmasking your inner dialogue, you will suddenly gain insight into the narratives that shape your self-perception. With practice, you'll transform self-criticism into self-compassion and self-doubt into self-confidence. This exercise is designed to foster a kinder, more positive relationship with yourself.

These two detective exercises will equip you with the investigative powers that you will need to recognize, understand, and later take charge of your thought patterns. As you hone your detective skills, you'll become adept at identifying the exact point in time that your mind starts to work against itself, enabling you to anticipate and pre-empt their attack on your senses. You will identify the thought culprits behind your negativity and proactively steer your mindset toward positivity. So, grab your magnifying glass, detective hat, and journal—it's time to uncover the amazing secrets of your mind!

As you embark on these exercises, remember that you're not just recognizing your thoughts; you're preparing to take back control of them. The "Recognize" phase is only the first act of your journey, and with these detective tools in hand, you're well on your way to becoming the master of your thoughts and the hero of your positivity. It's time to uncover the secrets of your mind!

Chapter Six

Principle #2: Explore

"The curious paradox is that when I accept myself just as I am, then I can change." [1]

Explore: Mining for Gold

Welcome to the next thrilling chapter of your journey, where you miraculously transform into a miner, mining your very own consciousness for those rich veins of self-understanding. The **"Explore"** principle is where you don your metaphorical miner's hat and shine a light around the hidden recesses of your mind.

---

1. Carl Rogers, (1956), 'This is me – The Development of my Professional Thinking and Personal Philosophy'

It's not for the faint-hearted, but it promises to reveal the hidden treasures and mysteries that shape your inner world.

Now, let's descend into "Explore" and the exercises that will illuminate the depths of your self-awareness:

Exercise 1: The Belief Explorer

Imagine yourself as an intrepid explorer of the mind, diligently digging away to uncover your deepest beliefs and thought processes. This exercise is all about delving into the why behind your thoughts and reactions. Here's how we will navigate these uncharted depths:

Mine the right vein:

We will begin by creating a dedicated section in your journal for the Belief Explorer. This will be your fifth column headed 'Beliefs ' and will serve to keep all your findings organized and in order.

The Question Quest:

Whether it's at the same time as your other observations or later on a given evening of the week with a large mug of tea in hand, I want you to pay close attention to your captured thoughts and emotional reactions. When you notice a recurring thought pattern or a strong emotional response, pause and ask yourself the best question possible, 'Why?' Why do you doubt your abilities in certain situations? Why do you feel anxious when facing specific challenges? And why does Mr Andrews from the second-floor office with the unusual collection of ties and immaculately polished loafers make you feel rather awkward? You are no longer a passive observer noting down what you feel and when you felt it as you did in the Recognize phase. This is now about creating a deeper form of self-understanding.

Digging for Treasure:

For each question, explore the outcome to a deeper level. Trace your beliefs back to their origins. Did a past experience shape your belief? Was it influenced by societal expectations, family upbringing, or cultural influences? This will require dedicated time to pause and think. This is also the moment for complete honesty with yourself. When the question why gives you an answer, seek further clarity by asking yourself why again. Keep descending in search of those golden nuggets of truth. Tunnel down into the layers of your beliefs like an archaeologist excitedly uncovering ancient artifacts. And when you have them note them down in your 'Beliefs' column.

Exercise 2: The Belief Map: Bringing it together

Your belief map will become a visual representation of the intricate web of your beliefs. It's like a mind map, but instead of charting concepts, you're exploring the terrain of your thoughts and convictions. To achieve this you will need to carve out about an hour of your time. Ensure that it's a quiet where you can focus without noise and distractions.

Here's how to create your very own Belief Map:

Mapping Materials:

To embark on this creative journey first gather together your materials. You'll need a large sheet of paper (A3 or larger, which peculiarly is called A2) or a digital canvas if you prefer a digital approach. You can also use colored pens, markers, or digital tools to make your map visually engaging. Don't worry, no Michelangelo's required for this exercise.

The Starting Point:

Begin with a central point on your piece of paper. This represents you and the epicenter of your beliefs. You can draw a simple stick figure, use your initials, or stick a picture there—whatever works for you.

Branching Beliefs:

Now, think of your beliefs as branches sprouting from the central point, you. These branches represent your core beliefs in your life. They could be related to self-worth, relationships, work, home, or any other significant aspect of your existence. This is where the previous exercise and those leading to it provide the input to your belief map. The golden nuggets that you have just mined act as your branches. It's important here that you strike a balance between negative and positive beliefs. Remember all the exercises relate to changes within yourself in both directions; things that add joy as well as things that add negativity.

Root Exploration:

As you extend these branches, imagine them reaching down through the soil of your experiences. Each branch connects to roots, symbolizing the origins of your beliefs. You can draw these roots as intricate patterns, each leading from the branch to a specific source or event.

Label and Reflect:

Alongside each branch, write a brief label to identify the core belief or the theme it represents. For example, if one branch relates to self-worth, you might label it as "Self-Worth Belief." Similarly, if a root connects to a childhood memory, such as "Schooling" label it accordingly.

Color Coding:

Consider using colors to categorize your beliefs or experiences. Assign a color code to different aspects of your life or emotions. For example, you might use red for negative beliefs, green for positive ones, and blue for neutral or ambiguous beliefs.

Curious Connections:

As you continue to build your Belief Map over time, you'll notice certain connections between branches and roots. Some roots might intertwine, indicating how past experiences shape multiple beliefs. These connections offer valuable insights into the complexity of your thought patterns. For example, a particularly painful event such as a marriage breakup may link to a belief of lack of self-worth as well as failure, and anger in certain situations.

Periodic Updates:

Your Belief Map isn't static; it's a dynamic tool for self-discovery. Periodically revisit your map and update it as you gain more insights into your beliefs and their root causes. You might use dashed lines to represent evolving beliefs or new branches to explore emerging themes.

Annotations and Reflections:

Alongside your map, consider adding annotations and reflections. Write down your thoughts and discoveries as you delve deeper into your beliefs. This will help you maintain clarity and understanding of your evolving belief system over time.

Compass of Self-Awareness:

Ultimately, your Belief Map serves as a compass through the labyrinth of your psyche. It provides you with a visual guide to your core beliefs and their sources. When you face challenges or seek personal growth, consult your map to navigate your inner landscape.

Creating your Belief Map is a transformative process. It allows you to visually grasp the complexity of your beliefs and the interplay between past experiences and your current mindset and responses. Your map will become a powerful tool for self-awareness and personal growth, helping you steer toward positivity and lasting change by recognizing the situations and circumstances that initiate emotional responses and their original source point.

So, grab your creative tools and start charting the fascinating interconnectivity of your beliefs!

Output:

Your Belief Explorer journal entries will reveal the underlying beliefs and thought processes that drive your reactions. You'll start to have a clearer understanding of why you think and feel the way you do in various situations. By taking this acceptance to the next stage and unearthing the origins of your beliefs, you gain the power to challenge and reshape them. You may also discover that many of your beliefs are based on outdated information or misconceptions. This exercise empowers you to navigate life with a renewed perspective driven by your introspective approach.

As you venture into the "Explore" phase, remember that you're embarking on a profound journey of self-discovery. Just like a miner digging for gold, you'll uncover hidden treasures and navigate the intricacies of your inner world. With these exercises, you're equipping yourself to understand the depths of your consciousness and emerge with a clearer sense of self. The "Explore" phase is your ticket to greater self-awareness and the path toward lasting positivity.

Chapter Seven

Principle #3: Shift

"To know yourself as the Being underneath the thinker, the still-ness underneath the mental noise, the love and joy underneath the pain, is freedom, salvation, enlightenment," [1]

⁂

Shift: The Perspective Shifter

Congratulations, intrepid explorers of your inner self! You've successfully dug down into the depths of self-awareness, mapping the intricate channels of your beliefs in the Explore phase. Now, as you resurface, imagine **"Shift"** as your seagoing vessel charting it's course to new perspectives and new lands fresh with positivity. It's time to see the world through new, vibrant lenses, like switching from an old black-and-white movie to a high-def

---

1. Eckhart Tolle (n.d.) As cited in James Jackson (2023) The +Point. The Power of Positive Thinking for Everyone!

blockbuster complete with Dolby 3D surround sound and a family-sized tub of popcorn. In this phase, we're not burying our heads in the sand or ignoring reality; we're simply embracing a more positive outlook and spotting opportunities where we once only saw insurmountable obstacles.

Exercise: The Three-Question Reality Check

Are you ready to shift your perspective with this simple yet immensely powerful exercise? Whenever you find yourself facing a challenge or feeling overwhelmed, grab your mental compass and ask yourself these three critical questions:

1. **Is this a catastrophe, or can it be managed?** Often, with the help of negativities mischievous grip manipulating our brains, we tend to magnify problems out of all proportions, turning molehills into monolithic mountains. The secret is to; Press pause, step back, and breathe. Once you have done that you can calmly and intentionally assess the situation objectively. Is it truly a catastrophe, or is there an easily manageable solution? Most of the time there is a solution. And know that Catastrophes rarely happen.

2. **What's the worst that could happen, realistically?** Our minds, having been kicked around by negativity, have a knack for conjuring worst-case scenarios that very rarely come to pass. Challenge these catastrophic thoughts by

asking yourself, "What's the worst that could realistically happen?" You'll likely find that the imagined horrors are far from reality even in the worst-case scenario. By rationalizing things down you can conquer those sudden feelings of overwhelm and fear.

3. **Are there any silver linings or opportunities in this situation?** This is the biggie. Instead of dwelling on the negative aspects, actively seek out the silver linings and potential opportunities. Is there a chance for personal growth, a lesson to be learned, or a hidden advantage that you haven't yet considered? Here's a tip for you based on my many years of observation; There is always a positive angle. Trust me. All you need to do is to have the willingness and fortitude to seek it out. Remember the comment about falling in a bucket of shit and coming out smelling of roses, well that is no accident. Well maybe the bucket part is, but if you go into things knowing that there is always a positive lurking somewhere inside a negative experience then all you need do is simply find it and exploit it. And guess what, you can do this!

By engaging in this three-question reality check, you'll quickly notice a shift in your perspective. You'll no longer be trapped and paralyzed in a gloomy, old movie; you'll be watching life in a full technicolor dreamcoat sort of way, with a newfound ability to see opportunities and solutions where you once saw only problems and roadblocks. This new-found perspective will set you apart from all those still dwelling in the dark with negativity as their only friend.

Output: The Power of Perspective Shift

This "Shift" phase isn't about living in denial or pretending that life is all sunshine and rainbows. It's about training your mind to recognize that challenges are a natural part of the human journey. In fact, if you subscribe to Agile working practices then failure is actually a form of success in its own right. It is simply ruling out one direction to focus the mind and your effort on another. Do you know how many attempts it took Space X to get a rocket to successfully launch? Four. That's three incredibly expensive failures that led the business to the verge of bankruptcy. The fourth attempt was fortunately a supreme success. As they say, "Shit happens". It just does but it's how you deal with it and what positives you create from it that count.

Through this exercise and a shift in your perspective, you will automatically gain a number of benefits:

- **Reduced Stress:** You will find yourself less burdened by catastrophic thinking and better equipped to manage the associated stresses as a result.

- **Enhanced Problem-Solving:** Your newfound perspective will improve your problem-solving skills, allowing you to tackle challenges with a clear mind whilst seeking positive resolutions.

- **Increased Resilience:** You'll become more resilient in the face of adversity, bouncing back from setbacks with a positive outlook.

- **Improved Decision-Making:** Your ability to make informed decisions will be enhanced as you focus on realistic outcomes and avoid spending time mourning the potential of failure.

The "Shift" phase is like upgrading your mental software, allowing you to approach life's challenges with optimism and confidence. Now let's progress to the next principle stage!

Chapter Eight

Principle #4: Embrace

"The secret of change is to focus all your energy not on fighting the old but on building the new." [1]

Embrace: The Positivity Nurturer

Fantastic work, positivity enthusiasts! You've traversed the realms of recognizing your thoughts, digging deep into exploration, and mastering the art of shifting your perspective. Now, picture "Embrace" as your daily gardening routine. Yes, I'm using yet another analogy. And this isn't your average slapdash gardening, oh no, it's a mindful and intentional process that you're undertaking here. You're not just tossing seeds randomly about

1. Dan Millman, (1980), "Way of the Peaceful Warrior"

and hoping for the best; you're meticulously tending to your positivity plants. Just like a skilled gardener, you'll nurture them with sunlight, water, and love every day, watching them grow and flourish. Each day contributes to their growth, just as each day of positivity contributes to your remarkable transformation.

Let's see where this line of thinking takes us.

Exercise #1: The Gratitude Garden

Welcome to your Gratitude Garden, where you'll cultivate the seeds of positivity and watch them bloom. This daily practice is like sunlight for your soul.

Here's how to get started:

Choose Your Moment:

Find a quiet moment in your day when you can focus without distractions. It could be in the morning with your coffee, during a lunch break, or before bedtime. Select a time that suits you best, making it a daily ritual.

The Blooming Process:

In your journal, create a dedicated section for your Gratitude Garden, heading it 'Gratitude'. Each day, I want you to list at least three things that you are grateful for. These can be simple joys or significant moments. The key is to focus on the positive aspects of your life. For example, you might be grateful for a kind gesture from a friend, a beautiful sunrise, or even a delicious meal that you didn't have to cook yourself. Ahh bliss!

Dig Deeper:

Don't stop at the surface level of that gratitude. After listing what you're grateful for, explore why each item brings you joy. What emotions do they evoke? How do they enhance your life? This deep dive into your feelings amplifies the positive aspect of the situation. Was the joy at your friend's kind gesture because you want to be more than just friends? Were the feelings from a beautiful sunset because it reminded you of a favorite time in your life? Was that delicious meal reminiscent of a moment of joy in a far-off place? What are your takeaways, no pun intended?

Exercise #2: Personalized Affirmations

Now you will recall that right at the start I listed the affirmation approach as being a bit lame and not really having a lasting effect. Well, there is no change in my thinking. The use of affirmation needs to reflect true life situations and your true life feelings associated with them to really stand up and make a difference over time. And here's how we are going to do it.

Affirmations with a Twist:

After your gratitude list, incorporate daily affirmations. These are powerful statements that reinforce both your positivity and self-belief. However, we're going to add a twist to these. Instead of generic affirmations, we will be crafting personalized ones based on your gratitude entries. For instance, if you're grateful for a supportive friend, your affirmation could be, "I am surrounded by caring and supportive friends who lift me up." If the sunset reminded you of a favorite time in life, say in the loving arms of your partner on a faraway beach then your affirmation could simply be "I know that I'm loved".

Visualize Growth:

Close your journaling session by visualizing your Gratitude Garden. Picture each gratitude entry in there as a vibrant plant, thriving and reaching skyward to the sun. See your affirmations as nourishing rain, helping your positivity garden flourish.

Output: Flourishing Positivity

The Gratitude Garden exercise is a bit like Jack and the Beanstalk. If you tend to your positivity plants in the right way, nurture, care for, water, and provide them plenty of sunlight by practicing gratitude and crafting personalized affirmations, they will grow to stratospheric proportions. In the process, you'll experience remarkable 'giant-sized' benefits including:

- **Increased Happiness:** Focusing on the positive aspects of your life cultivates happiness and contentment from within.

- **Greater Resilience:** Your daily rituals will enhance your resilience, helping you bounce back from challenges or other people's negativity.

- **Improved Self-Image:** Personalized affirmations boost your self-esteem and self-image, empowering you to embrace your true potential.

- **Mindful Living:** This exercise encourages mindfulness, keeping you present in the moment and aware of life's small joys.

As you nurture your Gratitude Garden, you'll notice that positivity becomes an ever-increasing natural part of your daily routine. Just as a well-tended garden flourishes, so too will your positivity, contributing to your remarkable transformation. So, grab your gardening gloves and let the sunshine of gratitude fill your days!

Chapter Nine

Principle #5: Transform

"Change is the law of life. And those who look only to the past or present are certain to miss the future." [1]

Transform: The Butterfly Effect

Congratulations! After recognizing your thoughts, digging deep into exploration, shifting gears, and nurturing positivity, it's time for the grand finale – transformation! Imagine this as your personal metamorphosis, much like a caterpillar becoming a butterfly, but without all those creepy crawly parts. Through your unwavering commitment to practicing and applying the principles of The +Point Process, you're about to embark on a profound journey of transformation. At the end of this journey, you will

---

1. John F. Kennedy,(1963) Address at the Assembly of the United Nations

emerge and take flight as a more resilient, optimistic, and pur-
pose-driven individual, ready to embrace life's challenges with a
newfound vigor for success.

So to one last exercise:

Exercise: The Positivity Scrapbook

In this exercise, you'll create a "Positivity Scrapbook" to visually
document your transformation journey. It's like crafting a personal success storybook that you can revisit whenever you need
a boost of homegrown positivity. Here's how to get started:

Gather Your Materials:

Collect together all the materials that you will need for your
scrapbook. You'll want a scrapbook or notebook, colored pens,
markers, stickers, glue, scissors, and any decorative items that
resonate with you such as inspirational quotes, magazine clippings, or photos. Yep, it's creativity time once again. For those
of you of a more technical disposition, you may wish to create
this on a digital canvas and avoid getting your fingers all stuck
together. The thing to bear in mind is that whichever direction
you decide to take, digital or physical, the end result will need to
be available to use whenever you need it.

Set the Stage:

Dedicate a quiet and comfortable space where you can work on your scrapbook. Make sure to create a positive atmosphere in which to work. That could be by listening to some meaningful or uplifting music or simply lighting a scented candle, whatever works for you.

Choose Your Pages:

Begin with a blank page in your scrapbook. This will form your "Transformation Timeline." On this page, create a timeline with milestones representing significant moments in your positivity journey. Leave space next to each milestone for descriptions and personal reflections.

Milestone Memories:

For each milestone, write a short description of the event or realization that marked your transformation. Include details like the date, location, and any people involved. Be honest and heartfelt in your descriptions.

Visuals of Victory:

Enhance your scrapbook with visuals. If you have photos from key moments in your journey, add them next to the corresponding milestones. Use markers and stickers to highlight positive quotes or affirmations that resonated with you during these moments.

Reflections and Gratitude:

Create dedicated pages for reflections and expressions of gratitude. Write about how you felt before your transformation and how you feel right now. Express gratitude for the lessons you've learned, the people who supported you, and the inner strength that you have discovered along the way.

Continuing the Journey:

Dedicate a section of your scrapbook to your ongoing positivity journey. Write down your aspirations, goals, and intentions for the future. It's a place to reaffirm your commitment to maintaining a positive mindset focused on creating the best opportunities for your success at home, at work, or wherever you may find yourself.

Decorate and Personalize:

Let your creativity shine as you decorate the pages of your scrapbook. Use colors, drawings, and decorations that resonate with your personal style and positive energy.

Regular Updates:

Make a commitment to regularly update your scrapbook. Set aside time each week or month to include new milestones, reflections, and positive experiences. Be sure to keep a focus on your goals and aspirations to keep them front and center of your efforts.

Share Your Story:

While your scrapbook is a personal keepsake, consider sharing it with a trusted friend or family member. If that feels uncomfortable then consider sharing some of the stories held within it. By sharing your journey with those around you, you can inspire others to take part whilst reinforcing your own commitment to positivity.

Output: Your Visual Transformation Story

Your "Positivity Scrapbook" will become a visual representation of your transformation journey. It's a tangible reminder of the progress you've made, the challenges you've overcome, and the positive mindset you've cultivated. Whenever you need a boost of motivation or a reminder of your resilience, flip through your scrapbook. It's your personal success storybook, showcasing the power of positive thinking in action along with the tangible results of success.

This exercise not only celebrates your journey but also reinforces your commitment to ongoing growth. It's a colorful and creative way to embrace your transformation and remain inspired, staying true to your path of greater positivity and personal success.

So, there you have it, my fellow passengers on the journey to positivity – the inner workings of The +Point Process. It's not just a catchy title; it's a transformative approach to creating a life more positive.

Now that we know the what, the why, and the how, let's examine the when and where as we plan out in detail your 28-day schedule to put these principles into action.

Chapter Ten

Preparation for Success

"The whole purpose of education is to turn mirrors into windows."[1]

Welcome to day one of the rest of your life. Over the course of the following 28 days, you will be putting into practice each of the five R.E.S.E.T. principles that we have explored in the proceeding Chapters. I will provide you with further information, the timings and context of each exercise, what they are designed to achieve, and when. Simples!

1.

Sydney J. Harris,(1957) "What True Education Should Do"

So make yourself comfortable, grab a cup of something hot, and be prepared to be taken on a thrilling journey of discovery as we head straight into the heart of our transformation journey. Grab your notepad, and let's go.

Preparing for Success

Welcome aboard, fellow positivity enthusiasts! We're about to embark on our 28-day adventure that will transform your life with The +Point Process. As we set off on this incredible journey, it's crucial to prepare for the days ahead. Picture this as gearing up for a cross-country road trip; you wouldn't hit the highway without a map, some snacks, and a killer playlist, right? Well, consider this chapter as your highway pit stop where you load up on all the essentials for a successful transformation trip. Is that Kylie Minogue CD?

Setting Realistic Expectations

Before we dive into the specifics of each RESET principle, let's talk about what to expect during your 28-day journey. Like planning a vacation, having realistic expectations is key because, let's face it, we're not in the business of selling magic wands. While The +Point Process is incredibly powerful, it's not a shortcut to overnight success or a magical cure for all of life's challenges. Sorry to disappoint you, but we won't be pulling rabbits out of overly-sized hats here.

Think of it this way: the first two RESET principles – Recognize and Explore– are your preliminary tools, like the warm-up exercises before the big game. They're your roadmap, guiding you toward the grand show that awaits further down the road. Your journey begins with recognizing the negative thought patterns that have been holding you back, exploring the depths of your mind to uncover hidden beliefs, and shifting your perspective to see the world in a new and more positive light. No shortcuts. You need to get this learned and under your belt as quickly as possible. And this we shall do.

Creating an Environment Conducive to Positive Change

Setting yourself up for success with The +Point Process requires creating an environment that fosters positive change that will support you until the end of your journey.

Here are some practical tips to ensure that your environment is conducive to positive transformation:

Clear the Clutter:

A cluttered space often leads to a cluttered mind where over-whelm is just an overbrimming filing cabinet away. Take the time to first declutter your physical surroundings to create a sense of order and calm. This is your home, your car, your workspace or office, indeed any place where you spend a lot of time. Hopefully, this is not a big task for you but if it is then I have recently had the pleasure to read an amazing book on the topic called "Home Decluttering Done Best for Success!" by Charity H Jones. If you need help in this area, then she's your gal.

Surround Yourself with Positivity:

Seek out and surround yourself with sources of positivity in your life. Connect with people who uplift you, read books that inspire you, and curate your social media feed to include content that motivates you. If you are feeling overwhelmed with work or life in general take some time out. Grab some fresh air, go for a walk, spend time doing your favorite things, or take up a new hobby. This may all sound rather simplistic but making sure that you are creating an environment that supports positivity around you is super important. It's far easier to swim with the current than against it, doubly so if you have a good pair of flippers on.

Daily Routine:

You are valuable, so treat yourself as such by making time for yourself. Establish a daily routine that incorporates time for self-reflection, gratitude, and personal growth. Like the above some quality downtime is key. Consistency is important here so establish this as a daily habit. Daily habit forming is often the key to success unless it includes forty Benson and Hedges.

Limit Negativity:

Identify and minimize sources of negativity in your life. In all likelihood, you will find negativity lurking around every corner, In your news feeds, social accounts, on the TV, and pouring from the mouths of many who have lost their own battle with negativity. The very fact that you will suddenly become attuned to this caustic outpouring will set you apart from your fellows. Your approach may include turning off the news, setting boundaries with negative individuals, and unsubscribing from negative channels. Like a great shampoo, you just need to wash all that negativity right out of your hair, or in this case your head.

Positive Affirmations:

Use positive affirmations strategically. Place them where you'll see them regularly – on your mirror, computer, or phone wallpaper – to remind yourself of your journey towards positivity. But remember affirmations only work if you 110% believe in them. To do that you need to craft them from your own experiences as explained earlier. Make them personal and real and you will be able to get behind them and stay with them for the long term.

By setting realistic expectations and creating a positively charged environment around yourself, you're laying the important groundwork for a successful 28-day transformation with The +Point Process. Think of this as your pre-trip checklist, ensuring that you're well-prepared for the exciting journey ahead.

Chapter Eleven

Day 1: The Power of Mindful Breathing

"If you want to conquer the anxiety of life, live in the moment, live in the breath." [1]

Alright, now that we've got our backpacks packed and our hiking boots laced up, it's time to hit the trail. Day 1 is like stepping onto the path of positive thinking for the first time, and we're going to start with a foundational practice – the power of mindful breathing.

---

1. Amit Ray (n.d.) As cited in James Jackson (2023) The +Point. The Power of Positive Thinking for Everyone!

Daily Exercise: Mindful Breathing

Our journey begins with something so simple yet profoundly effective – mindful breathing. This exercise is your passport to the Zen Zone, where your mindset reset adventure officially takes off. Mindful breathing isn't just any old warm-up; it's your superpower for keeping your cool no matter the situation. It will serve to keep you grounded and centered and it will be used throughout your 28-day adventure, and beyond. It's the art of being 100% present in the here and now, and here's how you will work your mindfulness magic:

An environment of calm:

Find a peaceful spot where you won't be disturbed. It could be in a quiet corner of your garden, a bedroom, or even a quiet park bench.

Sit Comfortably:

Take a comfortable seat, whether that's on a chair, a cushion, or even the ground. Keep your back straight but don't allow it to become too rigid. Allow your body to relax.

Close Your Eyes:

Minimize the distractions around you by closing your eyes.

Focus on your breathing:

Concentrate solely on the act of breathing. Feel your lungs inflate and deflate. Feel the air circulating within you as you draw it in through your nose and expel it from your mouth.

Breathe Naturally:

Simply observe your standard breathing. There's no need to alter it, just simply appreciate it as it flows in and out of your body. Notice its rhythm and pace.

Practice Mindful Awareness:

As you continue to breathe mindfully, become aware of any thoughts or emotions that arise. Don't try to engage or judge them just simply acknowledge their existence and let them drift by like clouds across the sky.

Set a Timer:

Begin with five minutes of mindful breathing, and then gradually increase the duration as you become more comfortable with the practice.

Think of the mindful breathing exercise as your daily 'reset' button. It helps you step out of the constant chatter of your mind and into the present moment. It's a practice that carries profound benefits, including reduced stress, and anxiety, and enhancing your overall well-being.

By beginning your journey with mindful breathing, you're setting a strong foundation for the days to come. It's like laying the cornerstone of a sturdy castle. With each mindful breath, you're fortifying your mental resilience, preparing to explore and shift your perspectives in the days ahead.

So, find your quiet space, take a comfortable seat, and let's dive into this practice. Day 1 is just the opening act of your transformative journey with The +Point Process.

Chapter Twelve

Day #2: Recognize

"Positive thinking will let you do everything better than negative thinking will."[1]

How did day one go?

Did you think, "What a cinch, he's just asking me to breathe, duh, I do that anyway!"

This is no kindergarten, breathing may sound fairly straight-forward but what about *'Mindful Breathing'* huh? Was that as straightforward? Did you take the time to fully relax and consider your thoughts of the day, allowing them to stream past without affecting your mood? Did you concentrate on yourself, on your breathing, your calmness, and your continued composure? Hopefully, you may have felt the weight of the world lift just a little as you took time purely for yourself. Yes? well, don't worry if you didn't, you have plenty of days to practice.

---

1. Zig Ziglar(n.d.) As cited in James Jackson (2023) The +Point. The Power of Positive Thinking for Everyone!

Now as surely day follows night, we enter the second day of training. This one will see us begin to get the basic principles of the R.E.S.E.T. framework in place.

You have already had a guided tour of the five key principles of the program; Recognize, Explore, Shift, Embrace, and Transform. Now we are going to put them into practice during your 28-day express ride to positivity.

Day 2: Recognize

Today we are going to concentrate on the first core principle of Recognize.

Hopefully, you have availed yourself of a journal of some kind and set it up ready to enter your observations. If not you can grab a pad of some description or nip over to my publisher's site where I have pre-designed a super simple sheet for you to use. It's free and if you are using Kindle or an e-reader you can find it **'Here'**, if you are enjoying the traditional paper version of this book then just hop, skip, and jump over to 3eyepublishing.com where you will find it at the bottom of the book description marked 'FREE'. A four-letter word we all like to see.

OK, so armed let's get the principle of Recognize started.

Thoughts on Paper

We will concentrate our efforts today on exercise #1. This is where you change your daily perception of yourself to include not just how you are dressed, do those shoes match your outfit, and oh my god just look at my hair! but also how you are actually feeling and more to the point when you notice those feelings suddenly start to change. This may well be a whole new experience that will take some time to get familiar with. We are all used to experiencing things such as frustration, happiness, anger, love, and indeed the whole smorgasbord of emotions, but taking notice of which mood you are entering at any given moment and why is something altogether quite different. It requires focus and a constant awareness of your emotional state which at first will seem quite foreign to you but, as with most things in life, it will get easier with practice.

So as you go through your day from waking to going back to bed I want you to be on the lookout for your emotional changes, both positive and negative. Remember to note them down as they happen along with what the trigger for the change was under two separate columns, headed 'Moods' and 'Triggers'. Get them all down on paper and safely secured in your journal for later review.

Here's a brief true-life story for you to highlight their importance:

One of my first ever jobs was to work for a very well-known retailer selling everything you can imagine all under one very big tin roof. I absolutely hated it. I used to wake up feeling depressed and anxious every workday. I would literally have to force myself out of bed and then once I had driven to work I had to summon immense courage to wrench myself clear of the car to start work. At that stage fear of what I would find and have to deal with would overwhelm me, handed the baton of negativity from my initial feelings of anxiety and depression that would accompany my first waking moments. Once inside it was pretty much a 50/50 chance that I would either have an averagely crap day or an utterly crap one. Needless to say, I left that job pretty quickly.

Now the point of my story wasn't to depress you but to show that every day I would have several challenges and associated changes to my state of mind that I could have recorded in my daily thought journal. These recordings would have provided me with the later realization that the universal denominator for my negativity was my god-awful boss. It wasn't my failures as a manager or indeed the failures of those poor souls who worked there or the customers or even the stock issues that we faced on a daily basis, it was just one person whose utter negativity passed from person to person like a bad case of Herpes.

Now hopefully you have not come across the same manager that I had all those years ago and life for you is not as depressing. But undoubtedly even just in the work environment, there will still be numerous occasions when you can take out your thought journal and scribble down your feelings and their triggers. Hopefully far more positive ones. This simple religious action will become really insightful especially as you continue to jot these down over the coming days and weeks. You will begin to see patterns of emotional behavior starting to jump out at you from the page. Some you will instinctively know, others you may have been consciously suppressing simply for an easier life and others may well be profound and utterly new. This is the very foundation of the +Point Process, driving clear and sustained self-awareness.

Now get to it and start recording.

Chapter Thirteen

Day #5: Talking Heads

"We are what we think. All that we are arises with our thoughts. With our thoughts, we make the world," [1]

No, you have not gone crazy. We have time-traveled forward to day five, thus giving you three whole days in between to practice using your Positivity Journal to capture your mood changes and their associated triggers. I also expect you to have been practicing your Mindful Breathing exercises to calm and center yourself along the road of discovery.

You may have already noticed a few repeating forms of behavior cropping up. The early signs of patterns forming from your notes.

---

1. Buddha, (n.d.) As cited in James Jackson (2023) The +Point. The Power of Positive Thinking for Everyone!

Now on day five, we will add a new and exciting exercise into the mix.

Welcome to Dialogue Diarizing.

Messing With My Melon Man:

This exercise will require you to listen carefully to the inside of your brain. Yes, you may not know this but your brain actually does speak. It has a voice, well several actually, all of its own. If you sit quietly and listen intently you can hear them deep in conversation. The only problem is that one voice likely belongs to Negativity. Remember that nasty little blighter, well he is lodged in there somewhere passed on by your fellow humankind and their own negativity-filled comments.

Think of it like a bad head cold. Easy to catch often a bugger to get rid of and always ends up with snot hanging between your fingers. Well, negativity can have a mighty loud voice to any argument going on inside there and if you have a severe head cold it will be negativity that wins every time.

Therefore think of this exercise like Lemsip.

Listening Intentionally

I want you to take some time out of your day to listen out for those arguments raging on inside your head, those utterances of self-doubt and trepidation. Once you have picked up on this inner dialogue I want you to write them all down into your journal. A word of warning, don't just listen out for the mental naysayers; we're interested in everyone present in this inner conversation. Your positive cheerleaders, the cautious skeptics, and even the dispassionate observers – they all have something important to say. This balanced 'eavesdropping' will prove to be invaluable as you continue with the process.

So, take a moment each day to listen closely to the inner dialogue and write them down in your journal next to your moods and triggers. Mark this one as Dialogues This deliberate introspection, this eavesdropping on your thoughts, will become a priceless tool as you continue on your transformative journey.

A Reflective Pause

As the day's journey winds down, it's the perfect time to reflect. Review the entries in your journal. Examine these thoughts and dialogues, pondering their accuracy in predicting your daily events. It's a moment for contemplation and understanding.

Ask yourself if they were a true reflection of your day or could there have been an entirely different outcome? Reflect and take it all in.

Each week review your recorded dialogues. Are they self-critical, self-doubting, or self-encouraging? Identify any recurring themes and the associated triggers that initiate these conversations. Start to compile a separate list for the 'Recurring favorites', creating a top ten for your recurring dialogue themes.

Challenge and Reframe:

For every self-critical or self-doubting dialogue you've documented, challenge its validity. Was it accurate or did things play out completely differently? Add another column in your journal for the reframed situation. Consider an appropriate reframe for the initial dialogue based on the actual output.

Here are a few combined examples to help:

You noticed that your mood shifted toward anger and frustration as you were informed by a work colleague that some tasks that you had requested to be undertaken during your absence were left unresolved. Inside your mind, Mr Negativity went straight to work. The dialogue within went something like this, "He doesn't respect you. He is undermining your authority. What other things has he not done in your absence". These all feel pretty negative and you respond in kind before your colleague can fully explain. Later that day you jot down these feelings – Anger and Frustration, along with the situation and the associated inner dialogue – "Mistrust, Undermined authority, and reduced credibility". Also later that day you discover that a number of your staff were off sick and that those remaining had to prioritize the more critical and urgent actions. You realize several things as a result. The first was that your initial assumptions driven by negative thinking were incorrect. The dialogue inside your mind was equally as incorrect and you need to redress your responses and ensure that you apologize to your colleague. The reframed dialogue that you now enter could be "My colleagues are trustworthy and resourceful and able to prioritize correctly without my support"

This exercise will reveal that, perhaps, the voices in your head don't always narrate reality. Some thoughts may seem exaggerated even a tad dramatic, or worse still, completely wrong. It's a subtle reminder that the mind enjoys crafting narratives, both real and fictitious, and perhaps the situation was not as bad as those nasty negative voices initially led you to believe.

Chapter Fourteen

Day #7: Belief Me

"To accomplish great things, we must not only act but also dream; not only plan but also believe." [1]

───────────❧───────────

Congratulations, you have managed to successfully reach the end of week one. I expect that it has been fairly enlightening already. You should be well on your way with the Mindful Breathing exercise and have a number of pages already filling up with your recorded mood changes and their trigger points. Next to these will sit your first couple of days of inner dialogue and their crafted reframes.

Have you overheard anything that you didn't already know? Have you identified how right or wrong those voices are? Have you discovered how manipulative the voice of negativity can be? How

---

1. Anatole France, (1881), "The Crime of Sylvestre Bonnard,"

he can twist your fears, uncertainties, and anxieties to any given situation? Is it already starting to become clearer?

Good.

Now we will introduce another exercise into the mix which if you have been paying attention you will already know as the Belief Explorer

---

The Belief Explorer

This exercise is taking the +Point Process to the next level, delving deeper into your belief process to uncover what lies beneath.

Now it could be a little early to start this exercise, but I can tell that you guys are quick learners and that you're eager to move on, so here goes. I want you to take a moment to explore any patterns that are starting to form in your journal entries.

Firstly you may find repeating patterns in your initial thoughts, such as always feeling nervous in the company of a certain individual. These may have transferred themselves to your inner dialogue. Could your reaction be because that person holds power over you, or that you greatly value their opinion and worry that they will not think kindly of you? Maybe you have noted down this same reaction to other situations with the same associated feelings that gnaw away at your self-confidence. Perhaps new patterns have started to emerge highlighting a difference between the dialogue and the reality of the reframed situation. Either way, I want you to ask yourself.....'' Why?''

Why are these repeating entries and associated themes starting to manifest themselves?

Why do you feel the way you do in certain situations?

Ask yourself if there are links to greater, deeper feelings, feelings that you have left submerged in the recesses of that wonderful brain of yours. Feelings that connect to others like loss or friendship or fear or love. Try to bring them into sharper focus bestowing on them greater detail. Going back to the example; Could your nervousness in certain situations and with certain individuals with power over you be more about your own need for praise and recognition than about them? Is that need born from a certain event or relationship either past or present? Explore your reactions and your beliefs to establish if they really represent the existing situations that you find yourself in or if this is just negativity rearing its ugly head and using your past experiences against you as part of your inner dialogue.

Explore until you feel that you have reached a full understanding of your belief. Once you have it, capture it in your journal under a separate column, entitled Belief, for later use.

Use the following week to get this three-stage process under your belt.

1. Capture and write down your feelings and their associated triggers.

2. Listen to the dialogue being played out inside your head. Capture it down and also check to see if it is a true representation of the situation or simply an irrational fear

that didn't really exist. Reframe them to reflect the truer situation and note that down too.

3. Finally, search deeper to establish why you feel and react the way you do. What were your beliefs that led you to those feelings? Identify any patterns that are forming and then delve deeper into those to establish if they are connected to something more deep-rooted.

Through this deeper level of introspection, you will start to discover the primary motivators of your responses. These are what Mr Negativity likes to use against you. An irrational fear of abandonment may well manifest itself as a negative response to any situation where a loved one is taking time apart from you, even if the reason for their absence is totally legitimate. A fear of failure may well surface as an irrational anger whenever anything goes wrong even when those occurrences are minor.

Only by following the process will you discover their legitimacy for yourself. I am not saying here that all deep-rooted fears can be magically eradicated from our lives just that by having a clearer understanding of our inner beliefs and the reframed dialogues based on the actual outcomes it will start to provide your brain with more positive expectations for future outcomes. Remember that your playdough will take time to remodel based on positive outcomes and self-inspection of our deeper beliefs. The good news – you have started that journey and it is only a matter of time before you reach your destination.

Chapter Fifteen

Day #14: Belief Mapping

"Believe in yourself and all that you are. Know that there is something inside you that is greater than any obstacle." [1]

———————— ❧❦❧ ————————

Two weeks down already. Wow! Your journal should be seeing a lot of action with all the noting down of mood changes, triggers, dialogues, reframes, and beliefs. This is where we ratchet things up another notch by taking all those learnings to a whole new level.

———————— ❧❦❧ ————————

1. Christian D. Larson, (1912),"Your Forces and How to Use Them,"

Belief Mapping

This is where you will discover your inner creative soul as we draw out a 'Mindmap' of your beliefs and convictions.

Gather your materials. You will need some colored markers and a large blank sheet of paper. Try A3. Starting with the blank piece of paper or if you prefer a more technical approach, a digital canvas, I want you to place yourself into its center. This can either be in the form of a photo or a drawing even just your name. From your image, I want you to draw branches stretching outward, one for each belief that you have discovered over the past couple of weeks. Make sure that each branch is clearly labeled. For instance, the belief could be "I am a failure", or "I am unlucky with relationships". Remember these beliefs should be a balance between positive and negative. You may have unearthed positive beliefs such as, "I am well-liked by my circle of friends", or "I am smarter than I think". Validate each one once again in your mind as you draw them out ensuring that they are a true reflection of your inner beliefs. Like all the exercises, it is important to be honest with yourself.

Now we will go a stage further as we explore the root causes that lie behind these beliefs. You may have already begun to explore these during the week which will give you a head start. If not then great we can work through this exercise here and now. These 'causes' will be represented on your page as roots extending away from the end of each branch. As you search deep and consider the root causes of your beliefs you may well find some repeating patterns between different situations and those related beliefs. If this is the case then you can connect these roots together. This will visually help identify the connections and the more deep-seated drivers for them.

To help with all this, let me provide you with an example;

Remember my torrid work-related example, where my top-level feelings included a toxic mix of fear, anxiety, and anger? These were the feelings that made my stomach churn, kept me up at night, and held me fast in the car seat before heading into the workplace. But if I consider why I felt that way it had more to do with my worry of failure, the work situation that I had found myself in, and the increasingly negative interactions I was having with my boss. Delving deeper, the beliefs that empowered those feelings included a fear that I lacked management ability, an underlying lack of self-worth, and an abject fear of failure and rejection. Each of these beliefs, had I drawn them onto a Belief Map, would on the surface be completely separate and would have been depicted as individual roots extending away from various branches. Even at that level, these discoveries would have provided me with a level of self-awareness that I could use to work with. However, through deeper introspection and searching right into the heart of the matter, I would have discovered that all those work-related situations that caused me so many negative feelings and sleepless nights were at the hands of Mr Negativity using my lack of self-esteem against me. Now that would have been a far more powerful insight to discover. And in reality, we all pretty much know what lies at the bottom of the well, don't we? We just need to take the time and the right actions to shine a light on them and call them out.

Now consider the huge positives that having that level of insight brings. You now know that a number of the occurrences that raise your heart rate and create feelings of fear, anxiety, and anger have nothing to do with the situation at all, but the fact that you relate those situations to your deepest beliefs which in my case at the time was a lack of self-esteem. Or spinning this around, if I didn't have insecurities about my self-esteem then all those situations related to it would have been viewed and dealt with in a far more positive and measured way. God, I wish I had read this book back then!

Now try this for yourself. The belief map will effectively visualize your thoughts and reasons allowing you to stand back and understand the interplay between past experiences and your current feelings and responses to certain situations. This is a truly powerful tool that enables you to identify the origins of your beliefs and to establish if those origins are current or historical.

Remember I have intentionally used a negative situation to highlight the benefits of the process but equally positive situations, raising positive feelings and beliefs with associated positive root causes will also be there in abundance. By conducting the same process with each of those situations you will be able to recognize, reinforce, and amplify the positivity that already exists in your life.

Now that you have captured the root causes you can confront them. Ask yourself if they should still hold sway over your emotional responses or if you could through greater understanding reshape them going forward.

In my case, it would have resulted in uncovering and highlighting an outdated belief, one which I could have worked through. I would have also established that the primary triggers for my negative feelings were centered on the outpourings of negativity and hostility from my then-boss and that they had nothing to do with my management skills or me as a person. These revelations would have equipped me with far greater self-understanding, resilience, and strength to address my own negative thinking as well as providing me an opportunity to address the root cause. My dealings with my ex-boss would have been less emotive and driven from a place of greater understanding with more appropriate and measured rational responses as a result.

Hopefully, this exercise will also lead you to uncover core truths to root causes that form your beliefs and which by understanding a little clearer can now be viewed, addressed and overcome.

Chapter Sixteen

Day #15: The Big 3 Questions

"Believe you can and you're halfway there." [1]

———— ❧❦❧ ————

We are already halfway through the 28-day +Point Process and we have spent the first few weeks moving from preparation through Recognition and into Explore, two of the five RESET Principles. These have focused primarily on the task of understanding ourselves a whole lot better and in doing so created a rock-solid foundation on which to build our successful, more positive futures, with the help of the next three Principles, Shift, Embrace, and my favorite of all, Transform.

Think of the +Point Process as being quite linear, set across three timeline phases; Your past self, your present self, and, yes you

---

guessed it, your future self. Or breakfast, lunch, and dinner for all you foodies out there. We have done with breakfast and now we are sitting down for a nice spot of lunch with the next exercise, The big 3 questions.

Question Introduction

This is a great exercise and I use these three questions whenever a situation goes a little astray. By applying these on a daily basis or whenever there is an overwhelming situation at hand you will be better able to positively frame the issue and its resolution more accurately. The process will aid your path from emotionally driven responses to more pragmatic, rationally driven ones.

Let's try them out:

Question #1: Is this a catastrophe, or can it be managed?

As mentioned, it is rare that any given situation can be accurately classified as catastrophic. Although our minds would have it not so. Whenever there is a negative situation such as a personal confrontation, a plan that falls through, or simply when something doesn't go right, our minds immediately whirr into action, and our enemy Mr Negativity gets stuck into our inner conversations. We can instantly be persuaded to see the worst of things. But having paused, taken a breath, and really thought through the situation, you will be in a far better place to determine its true severity. Is it a catastrophe *really* or, now that we are taking time to rationally approach the situation, can it be managed and controlled?

Question #2: What's the worst that could happen, realistically?

It's rarely ever going to be the worst-case scenario. Rationalizing the situation down to a number of likely outcomes allows you to focus on alternatives whilst negating your initial fears and overwhelm. This also introduces problem-solving into the mix rather than simple acceptance of a bad situation. This shift in perspective allows you to introduce positive thinking ready for the next big question.

Question #3: Are there any silver linings or opportunities in this situation?

Now you have moved out of the negative arena and are searching within the positive realm for solutions and benefits. How can you reshape the situation to form positive outcomes? Now you have entered problem-solving mode, focused on making the best of the situation at hand. Seek and ye shall find! Your mind will welcome the switch from negativity to positivity.

Here's a tip, there is almost always a positive to be found in every given situation, trust me. You just need to search hard enough to find it. And do you know what else is good about this direction of thinking? Others around you will suddenly be more enthusiastic to help search for the best positive outcome too.

Basically, people prefer success to failure, so collaborating to find solutions is an ideal way of finding shared purpose and camaraderie.

Now do you see where this is heading?

Shifting Gears

Having gained an understanding of your dialogues and beliefs along with their root causes enables you to reframe them, shifting them from emotive negatives to more acceptable and more positive considerations. By doing this you have suddenly regained control of your responses. Negativity no longer holds sway in your brain. You can begin to look at things in a more rational and positive light, finding acceptable outcomes in less-than-optimal circumstances. At the same time, you have successfully identified your positive beliefs and gained an understanding of what drives those within yourself. This enables you to utilize those positive beliefs in an array of similar situations. This readdressing of the balance between negative and positive thinking will start driving successful outcomes to situations that otherwise would have been seen as failures, even catastrophic ones.

Let me provide you now with a positive example from my own past:

After escaping over the wall from the retailer that won't be named, I found myself supporting the home furniture sector back in the good old UK. Now this was a far better career move with a great team of managers and co-workers supporting me who in general all worked in a very positive, fully empowered, and may I say, highly successful way. This was more like it! However, there was still one dark cloud on what was otherwise a blissfully sunny day. One part of this two-billion pound enterprise held many of the others back. It impacted the whole business but was at the same time seen as a powerful force within the organization. Unfortunately in my numerous dealings with them, I had only found negativity, delays, and roadblocks in a bid for them to maintain their overly tight controls.

This came to a head over one specific alternative approach that I wanted to try out. This independent and novel method of trying new things out and seeing how they would land was immediately frowned upon even after much research was done to make many people feel far better about themselves. Now I and those around me instinctively knew that this new approach, backed by sound research data, would work, and therefore after several attempts at negotiating an amicable way forward, I just went ahead and initiated it.

We won't go into the specifics only so far as that I took a reasonable risk in breaking the stranglehold of a negative part of the business based on my belief and it proved itself successful in every possible measure. This paved the way for further breakthroughs and for the eventual transformation of the negative part of the business that had existed unchallenged for so long.

Now that is not the main positive from the story. You see, as my career developed I always fondly remembered the success of that moment. My mind had learned that it was OK to challenge existing dogma and find new ways of doing things in a proactive way, and if unreasonable resistance still remained then it was OK to circumvent it and do it anyway. I had trained my mind to think positively and outside the traditional guard rails that existed in whichever business I would later find myself in. It also helped significantly with my self-esteem issues and empowered me to live by the proverb, ***"It's better to ask for forgiveness than to wait for permission"***

Positivity Epidemic

By incorporating these learnings which are taken from your experiences you will start to realize a new positive you. It may be slow at first and take practice but just as you are able to identify the negative influences on your reactions, you can also nurture the positive ones too. And remember these can be from and applied to, any situation at any time under any circumstances. Training your brain to focus on the positive rather than the negative is habit-forming and self-sustaining leading to ever more successful outcomes.

As this new more positive you enter's into conversations with others, you will act like a vaccine to their head colds of negativity. You will be able to kick-start their brains into a positive mode to enable collaborative working and bring about successful outcomes. Positivity feeds positivity just like the inverse is true. By using the +Point Process you will not only be making a huge difference to yourself but also to those around you. I have seen it happen time and time again and know that one individual can light the path to positive thinking for the rest to follow creating a powerful positivity epidemic.

Now let's move even further along the +Point Process to the next stage of our journey.

Chapter Seventeen

Day #21: Positive Gratitude

"Gratitude is the sign of noble souls." [1]

Now you are really motoring on! Your journal is quickly filling up, you have a fully drawn-up mind map of your beliefs and root causes, you are tackling challenging situations with your Jedi understanding of the big three questions and you are starting to feel the difference in your approach to life. It's also likely that those around you are starting to notice the more positive you. This is now the moment when we attune ourselves to all the positive impacts happening around us with the Gratitude exercise.

---

1. Aesop (n.d.) As cited in James Jackson (2023) The +Point. The Power of Positive Thinking for Everyone!

The Gratitude Exercise

This exercise focuses on developing your positive mindset through another daily practice that I want you to introduce into your regime. This one will take no more than 10 minutes each day and will need to be done when you have peace and solitude around you, ideally late evening. I want you to sit back and open your journal. Read back through the entries of your day. Reflect upon the valuable information that you have diligently captured. Intentionally focus on the positive things that have been recorded. Create a separate section headed 'Gratitude' and challenge yourself to think of three things that you are grateful for from your day. Don't just include any old thing here to get the exercise done, I want you to really take the time to consider what are the three main things that you are grateful for. Before you enter them into the journal dive deeper into the why. Why are these the three items of gratitude? What emotions did they trigger? Does it relate to something far deeper? Don't enter something unless you can feel some real emotional connection to it because it just proves that it wasn't significant enough to attribute gratitude to.

Here's an example; when collecting your young son from school his teacher comes over to you and joyfully tells you how well he has been doing in class. This is a perfect gratitude moment to capture in your journal. Their praise for your son creates an immense sense of gratitude, pride, and thankfulness. But beneath that, lies a deeper level of gratitude. Gratitude for your son's development and for the proof point that your parenting skills are having a genuine positive effect on his development. There may well also be gratitude toward the teacher who went out of her way to find you and provide you with positive encouragement based on your son's performance. That form of gratitude could be for confirming that your son has a highly supportive teacher who will go out of her way to keep you appraised of his progress.

Having captured the three moments of gratitude I want you to also write down the emotions that these bring. Be it pride, joy, or whatever the emotion is. It will embolden the meaning behind the gratitude that you are expressing and make it a living entity in your mind. Something you can both read and feel simultaneously.

Gratitude Affirmation Exercise

This is an additional follow-up activity that you can do. Having collected all those gratitude moments and their related emotions, I now would like you to form them into personalized affirmations. These will go with the rest of the affirmations that you have been curating. These positive statements will serve to reinforce and sustain your positive mindset, self-worth, and self-belief.

Using the example above the affirmation could read; "I am a great mom, doing a great job!". Try to come up with at least one personalized affirmation every day and when you enter it into your journal remember to read all the previous ones that you have entered. Visualize all these statements as proof points of the abundance of positivity that surrounds you day in and day out.

Chapter Eighteen

Day #28: The Butterfly Effect

"We delight in the beauty of the butterfly, but rarely admit the changes it has gone through to achieve that beauty," [1]

And just like that four weeks have flown by.

Your journal is fit to burst, your mindset has shifted from negative to positive, you can tackle challenges head-on to find the best possible outcomes and you have learned to provide gratitude and affirmations to inspire you for the long run. You should congratulate yourself for all the effort that you have put in to get this far. Go on, stick the kettle on, and grab yourself a Ginger biscuit. But wait, hold on, there is still more to do. We need to address the last RESET Principle in the +Point Process. We need to enter the world of transformation.

Positivity Scrapbook

Think of this exercise as Lucazade for your positivity. It is designed to enable you to recognize the fantastic positive journey that you have been and continue to be on. It also acts as a booster to your positive mindset every time you interact with it.

The positivity scrapbook exercise is where you rekindle your relationship with your creative side. Grab yourself all the materials that you could ever need to create a scrapbook from scratch; pens, markers, stickers, scissors, inspiring quotes, magazine clippings, and photos. The idea of the positive scrapbook is to visualize your journey via a timeline, from day one to twenty-eight, but remember to leave space for your continuing journey. Add images that capture your positive journey and quotes that sum up learnings and experiences. Include notes or annotations that bring to life the emotional changes that you have witnessed. Draw your own images if you like, anything that visualizes the moments that stand out.

Take time to refer back to your journal for inspiration. Reflect on the five core principles of the +Point Process; Recognize, Explore, Shift, Embrace, and Transform. Think about the exercises attributed to each of these stages of the process and the outputs that you have gained from each of them. From the first day when you simply took time to breathe and mindfully concentrate on yourself and your well-being, to the first feelings that you noted down, the triggers, the beliefs, the reframes, the mapping exercise, and the deeper meaning that lay behind your emotional responses. Now think of the moment that you shifted gear, allowing yourself to enter the realm of positivity, battling against negative feelings irrespective of the situations that you found yourself in. Think of the first time that you asked yourself the three big questions and how you learned to reframe a problem into a solution, a failure into a success. And finally onto those moments of positive gratitude and affirmation to help empower your positive thinking ongoing.

Bring all of those wonderful moments to life in a visual buffet lovingly captured in your scrapbook. And once it's complete don't just put it to one side and say 'job done'. Keep it to hand, add further entries as time passes, and keep on referring back to it to relive the feelings of success that you have created.

Now consider those around you, your family, loved ones, work colleagues, and friends. How has their behavior toward you changed? Have they commented on your new more centered approach to life and the upswell of positivity that now surrounds you? Have they begun exhibiting the same positive traits? Is your newfound attitude becoming contagious? It's still early days, twenty-eight of them will not change your life instantly but consistency and staying the course will.

You now have the power of positive thinking a power that will set you on the path to ongoing success, at work, at home, and wherever you find yourself. Now you are 'that' person, the one that friends, colleagues, and loved ones will reach out to in a moment of need because they will hear the whispering voice that says "You've got their back".

Chapter Nineteen

Day #29: The inflection point

"This is how willpower becomes a habit: by choosing a certain behavior ahead of time, and then following that routine when an inflection point arrives"[1]

Surprise!

There is a very good reason why my carefully crafted 28-day transformation training program has 29 days in it. No, It's not because it's a leap year, but more to the fact that is going to be a 'great' year! Think of this chapter as the special advanced training for all of you who have dedicated the last four weeks to completing the program.

---

1. Charles Duhigg, (2012), The Power of Habit: Why We Do What We Do in Life and Business"

Earlier on I discussed why I had named the process the +Point. The plus was to reflect the topic of positive thinking and the 'point' was to signify the moment that you should put your learnings into practice. Now over the last 28 days you have spent a lot of time on introspection, shifting perspectives, understanding when negativity can affect you, and what you can do to stop it. But what if you could anticipate it before it even happened and preempt the situation altogether?

Now that would be cool right?

Not only would you be armed with all the understanding of why you react in the way that you do, and what to do when those situations occur but you would be able to use that knowledge before those situations even arose. It's like 'The Time Traveller Wife' without Eric Bana getting shot at the end – ops spoiler alert if you haven't seen the movie yet.

Let's now have a look at this intriguing opportunity.

What's the Point?

Consider all those times that you have looked back at a situation and thought, "I wish I hadn't said that", or, "I wish I hadn't reacted in that way", or simply, "Shit!". How many arguments or misunderstandings could you have avoided through your life so far if you had only changed your approach or not bitten back at a certain remark? Mine, like many, would be in the thousands I am sure. Generally, when we do reflect on those types of situations we attempt to rationalize them or shift the blame to the other person, or the particular circumstances, but deep down we know that we could have done better. We could of been better. This is the true meaning of the "+" in the process title. I'm sorry that you had to wait until now to fully explore it, however, you needed to have completed the rest of the training to gain the greatest benefit from it. Yes, there is a method in my madness.

Column zero

So how can we bend time and assert our newly gained super-powers of positive thinking before a situation that requires it even occurs? That is a great question and I already knew that you were going to ask it. I am going to provide you with the life-changing solution. It involves column zero. This is the column that has yet to be squeezed into the front of all the other columns that I asked you to create in your journal. Now if you had been resourceful and had initially headed over to the free journal page download **here** or at **3eyepublishing.com**, you would now know that the sheet was not, as you first thought, really badly made, but was in fact waiting for this precise moment to be correct. And if you made your own journal columns then, sorry but squeeze this one into the margin.

Consider column zero as the receptacle of your 'lead up' and the most important column of them all. These are the feelings that you experience as negativity starts to climb down your left ear to fiddle with your brain. The run-up to those feelings of negativity before they have had a chance to have a conversation with your mind. Think of it like a surfer feeling the swell of the sea rise beneath them before paddling like fury and jumping up on the board.

I want you to start to attune your mind to feeling those moments as they occur. The moment when a discussion with your partner starts to diverge into a disagreement, the times when you're in a meeting and you start to feel the first prickles of anxiety, or the point where your heartbeat accelerates when confronting a neighbor. These are all tale-tale signs that negativity is about to pounce. Write down and capture those feelings as soon as you experience them in column zero.

Pattern forming

Over the following weeks try to capture as many of those 'lead-up' feelings and sensations as possible. Now don't worry if you miss a few at first as this is not an easy thing to do. But over time you will get more adept at tuning into those emotions as they start to arrive. Look out for them in the minuscule happenings within your being. It could be a slight temperature rise, a flushing of the cheeks, faster-paced breathing, a lack of focus or simply withdrawing from a conversation and failing to listen. Note them all down and then at the end of each week I want you to reflect upon the list to establish if patterns are forming. Are there any connected indicators of negativity before it messes with your melon? Once you find them pull them out and either highlight them or write them down separately along with the situations in which they occurred. Now the great news is that because you have been following the full +Point process, not only do you have the trigger, the feelings, and the situation but you also have the dialogue, the belief, the reframe, the affirmations, etc. all neatly captured down providing you with the 'what-happens-next' information. It's basically like knowing the future ahead of time. It's the instant replay before the play.

Changing the point of Inflection

Just think what a boon it would be to know the future ahead of time when it comes to your interactions. Although I guess attending Murder Mystery nights would be pretty pointless now.

Here's a time-bending scenario to help demonstrate this miracle in action:

You have been asked to put a presentation together for an important meeting and your boss wants you to run through the deck with him before you present it. You begin showing the slides and he starts to interrogate the information and the presentation flow. You start to feel the first signs of mood change. You are feeling flushed and are starting to talk quicker as you try to move the presentation on to avoid further discussions.

This is the point of inflection.

Based on experience, negativity will be about to swing into action with feelings of frustration, uncertainty, and mild forms of irritation He will start by telling you that your boss is a jerk and that he should have provided the information himself if he was worried that you would present the wrong facts. Then as the dialogue intensifies inside your brain you will start to close down to any input that your boss may have, as you hear from within, "He doesn't have confidence in you" or "Your presentation sucks". You also know from past introspection that negativity is using your 'Need for recognition and praise ' against you and that this belief is linked to a far deeper feeling of low self-esteem. So you know all the negatives and the reasons why you will start to feel that way but you can also reflect upon the positives.

From studying past experiences you discovered that your presentations were viewed as high quality and that you always got a great response from your audience. Your affirmations tell you that 'You are an inspiring presenter who knows what you're talking about.' Suddenly you begin to feel a lot calmer and more self-confident. You recall that several of your gratitude statements refer to 'support from colleagues to help you grow and thrive'. Now you can start to see the benefit of your boss's input and that it could help to make this your best presentation yet.

All of the above internal processing happens in your helicopter-fast brain which means that you return to the precise same point in time where you have two choices at hand;

Choice #1: To follow the same path as you have done before that ended in highly defensive conversations, heated discussions, and raised voices, or

Choice #2: Decide on a new path and a change of tack where you steady your breathing, slow down your discussions, reflect on the input, and seek ways to incorporate it to make the presentation flow better and be more accurate.

You decide which route you would take.

If you chose option #2, you would have changed the inflection point, effectively rewriting the future more positively.

More to the Point

Once you start to place all the pieces together and begin pre-empting situations you will be using the +Point force to its full potential. The power will be strong within you and the padawan would have become the master of their reactions by reframing the outcomes before they even happen. Now all you have to do is repeat this exercise whenever you feel those early indications of negativity approach. And the great news is that the more you do it the stronger you will grow those neural pathways and the more it will become second nature to you.

Each time you are successful at changing the inflection point you should include the details into your Positivity Scrapbook so that you can sit and reflect upon your amazing transformation. This, in itself, will reaffirm the abundance of positivity that now resides within you. This is what I call the virtuous circle of Positivity, one in which each action empowers the following action driving ever more positive outcomes.

Congratulations you have completed the +Point Process!

Chapter Twenty

Overcoming Challenges

"The only thing that stands between you and your dream is the will to try and the belief that it is actually possible,"[1]

Welcome to our continued exploration through the wondrous realms of positivity and self-discovery. You have successfully completed the +Point, so why, do you ask, are there still five more chapters? Well, there are a number of situations that you may encounter as you work through the +Point Process which I want to make sure that you are prepared for. Think of these as additional strategies to get you and keep you on the path to positive thinking.

---

1. Joel Brown (n.d.) As cited in James Jackson (2023) The +Point. The Power of Positive Thinking for Everyone!

Cultivating Positivity in the Face of Life's Challenges

As you continue your journey with The +Point Process, you will have already fortified your defenses against negative self-talk as it happens. Now, it's time to delve even deeper into the art of navigating challenges with grace and resilience. Life throws curveballs at us, but with the right mindset, you can not only face them head-on but also thrive.

Acknowledge the Challenge:

Always start by acknowledging the challenge that you are currently facing. Whether it's a personal setback, a difficult relationship, or a professional obstacle, name it and write it down in your journal.

Analyze Your Initial Reaction:

Reflect on your initial emotional response to the challenge. What were your thoughts and feelings when it first appeared in your life? Jot these down next to the challenge. It's important to be honest with yourself. We all have go-to emotional reactions to certain situations, the key is to use that understanding to shape more positive and successful reactions for the future. Were your reactions based on past experiences? Were those past experiences a true reflection of the final outcome? Or were your responses just out of habit? Take a moment to think these through carefully.

The +Point Connection:

There are two principal exercises that you should consider in this situation.

1. **Positive affirmation attribution:** The first exercise is positive affirmations. Throughout your time with the program, you will be creating positive personalized affirmations based on certain situations and occurrences. Search through your journal to see if any can be applied to this new situation. If none quite fit then resort to remembering positive outcomes that you have managed to reach from an assortment of negative situations. There will be one that lends itself to the new situation.

2. **Reframe Your Perspective:** With your affirmations in mind, I want you to now ask yourself the big three questions to reframe the challenge (see Chapter 16). Look for ways in which this particular obstacle can contribute to your personal growth, wisdom, or resilience. Are there hidden opportunities held within it? Write down your newly reframed perspective.

Plan of Action:

Develop a plan of action based on your reframed perspective. What steps can you take to address the challenge positively? Are there other people who can be involved in the resolution process? What is their motivation and can you aid that motivation from a positive mindset perspective? Set clear, achievable goals and deadlines to address it. By taking these steps you will reduce the emotional stressors and increase your logical reasoning quotient.

Daily Practice:

Incorporate this reframe exercise into your daily routine. Use it whenever you face moments of doubt or frustration related to a challenge. Use it as a source of motivation and resilience to relook at the situation and find a successful path.

By practicing "The Reframe," you're actively training your mind to see challenges as stepping stones rather than stumbling blocks. Remember that you already possess the strength and wisdom to overcome them, and your affirmations and previous positive experiences are your unwavering supporters.

Real-Life Stories of Triumph

To further inspire and empower you, let us explore a couple of real-life success stories. Let's turn our attention to individuals who faced daunting challenges and emerged stronger, wiser, and more resilient in the process.

Malala Yousafzai – A Champion of Resilience and Positivity

Malala Yousafzai's journey to becoming a beacon of resilience and positivity began in Swat Valley, Pakistan. As a young girl, she defied the Taliban's oppressive ban on girls' education and advocated for their right to learn. This fearless stance placed her in grave danger. In 2012, a Taliban gunman boarded her school bus and shot her in the head. Malala miraculously survived this brutal attack, and her unwavering commitment to her cause only strengthened.

After her recovery, Malala continued her activism, speaking at the United Nations and establishing the Malala Fund, a non-profit organization dedicated to girls' education worldwide. Her extraordinary efforts gained her the Nobel Peace Prize in 2014, making her the youngest-ever recipient at the tender age of just seventeen.

Malala's story exemplifies the extraordinary power of resilience in the face of adversity. Her unwavering belief in the transformative power of education, even when confronted by violence and oppression, underscores the core principles of positive thinking. She embodies the idea that challenges, no matter how daunting, can be reframed into opportunities for personal growth and global impact.

Thomas Edison – The Inventor of the Light Bulb and the Eternal optimist

Thomas Edison's journey to inventing the light bulb was a testament to his unwavering optimism and relentless pursuit of innovation. Edison was no stranger to setbacks and failures; his most famous quote, "I have not failed. I've just found 10,000 ways that won't work," encapsulates his perspective on adversity.

Edison's path to the electric light wasn't a linear one. He conducted many thousands of experiments resulting in what others would consider failures. Yet, he viewed each unsuccessful attempt as a step closer to his ultimate goal. His boundless optimism allowed him to maintain focus and determination throughout this arduous process.

In 1879, Edison finally succeeded in creating a practical, long-lasting electric light bulb, a groundbreaking invention that transformed the world forever. His story showcases how a positive mindset can not only drive personal success but also reshape the course of history. Edison's remarkable journey demonstrates that when you see challenges as opportunities and approach them with unwavering optimism, you can achieve the seemingly impossible.

Both Malala and Edison's experiences serve as powerful examples of how positivity and resilience can lead to remarkable personal and global change. By internalizing the principles of "The +Point" Process, you too can adopt their mindset, turning challenges into stepping stones towards a far brighter future.

Chapter Twenty-One

Overcoming Setbacks

"Our greatest glory is not in never falling, but in rising every time we fall." [1]

Beyond challenges lie setbacks.

Now, I don't want to worry you, but there will be times, not many but times, when things do go wrong, despite all your best efforts to maintain your positivity and rescue the outcomes. No one wants setbacks, but here's the key: it's not about the setbacks themselves; it's about how you deal with them. And guess what? That's exactly what we're going to explore here.

---

1. Confucius (n.d.) As cited in James Jackson (2023) The +Point. The Power of Positive Thinking

Navigating Life's Twists and Turns

Imagine life as a winding path, filled with unexpected twists and turns. Most of these will bring joy and delight, others will have neutral outcomes, while very few may lead you into rough terrain, where the path is obscured by heavy rain, storms, and even deafening thunder. Now no one likes to be out in a thunderstorm without a jacket. I'm English so we always carry an umbrella even in the height of summer, just in case.

This is where your resilience comes into play. Resilience isn't about avoiding setbacks; it's about responding to them with unwavering positivity. In short, consider this Chapter as your golf-sized umbrella for life's stormy times.

Constructive Self-Reflection

Okay, so something that you are responsible for has gone badly wrong. This could be a relationship, a family matter, a dealing with a friend, or a work-related issue. Whatever the situation or the cause of the 'catastrophe', if it really is one, there will always likely be a solution. The very first thing not to do is panic. This is our go-to response when something calamitous happens. We have been trained by ourselves and others over time and circumstances to seek out negative thinking and try to hang, draw, and quarter ourselves before anyone else can get the opportunity. We are pre-programmed to imagine the worst and relive it time and time again in our imaginations until we feel utterly miserable and unable to do anything else but resign ourselves to our fate. **DON'T DO THAT!** That is what negativity wants you to believe and wants you to do. He has got you by the short and curlies and is eager for you to suffer. This is negativities home turf, it's where he sharpens his teeth and feasts on his victim's misery. Don't provide him with another meal, not even a merest morsel.

This is what you do. You take a mindful breath. Then you take another, and you keep on taking another until you can calm your mind and move from the emotion of the moment to a more logical standpoint. Then calmly you are going to undertake the next exercise.

Exercise: Constructive Self-Reflection with "The +Point" Process

Together we are diving deep into the art of constructive self-reflection, a crucial skill for maintaining your positivity, especially when facing setbacks. The +Point Process that you have been diligently practicing will now become your trusty compass in these stormy seas.

Recognition:

Start, as always, by honestly and rationally recognizing the setback that you are facing. Write it down clearly. Remember to enter all the details that make it a calamity in your mind. Now reflect on all the setbacks and challenges that you have met on your entire journey with this program. What challenges have you faced? What obstacles have you tripped over? What learnings have you gained? Take a moment to write them down in your journal, acknowledging their presence. If you have yet to meet a setback during the process then search further back in your mind to when you have and what you have done to confront it. Focus on those that brought a successful outcome.

Exploration:

Now, let's explore these setbacks through the lens of The +Point Process. What did you learn from these experiences? How have they tested your resilience and belief in yourself? Most importantly, what positive aspects can you extract from these seemingly negative events? What did you do? What did you find? It's important that you approach this exercise honestly searching for the key positive outtakes that you will take forward to your next action. Remember to capture them by writing them down. Consider which of these can be applied to this particular situation.

Shift:

Assuming that the 'catastrophe' has either happened or is imminent then you are likely searching for mitigation solutions. If the event could be diverted then this needs to be treated as a challenge and not a very rarely occurring setback.

Next, apply the 3 big questions but in this instance, adjust them slightly to read:

Question #1: Is this a complete catastrophe or can elements of it be managed and mitigated?

You may find that by rationally asking yourself this question you can reframe the event and find that it is more of a challenge than a setback. Perhaps taking a more rational approach to the situation can avert it from calamity. If so immediately revert to the previous Chapter. If not, ask yourself if there are any elements of it that can be managed or mitigated.

Here is an example; A project may have failed at work. Sales that were dependent upon it have not materialize and the project is to blame. Ask yourself if there were elements of the project that did work even if the overall result was disappointing.

Now you are moving from a negative outlook with a resigned acceptance mindset to a more curious one that actively seeks to reduce the impact of the event in question. As soon as Mr Negativity gets to work on our brains we can quickly be persuaded to see the worst of things. But having paused, taken a breath, and really thought through the situation, you will be in a far better place to determine its true level of severity.

Question #2: What's the worst that could happen, realistically?

To you, this failure may seem catastrophic, but is it really? Consider other people's perspectives on the subject and their knowledge of the event. Do they see it in the same way? Think through the event clearly and positively. Don't just think of the worst-case scenario but also consider the best-case outcome. Try to come somewhere close to the middle ground when considering likely outcomes. Can you move the outcome to a more positive point? What needs to happen for that to be achieved?

Question #3: Are there any silver linings or opportunities in this situation?

Now Positive thinking comes in to save the day. You are problem-solving with a positive outlook and a growth mindset, moving a catastrophe into a managed crash landing as it were. What positives are there to explore?

Going back to our project example; Can the elements of the project that worked provide data that could indicate that these aspects could make money in the future? What exact parts of the project failed and what learnings can be gained to avoid the same mistakes happening again? Can a reworking of the project perhaps focused on different deliverables be successful? Or could you focus purely on the elements that did work? The power of positive thinking even in the worst situations is that you are looking for solutions rather than accepting failure.

If a relationship is lost can a friendship be saved? If money has been lost can it be recovered over time? These as well as many other examples showcase the change in mindset to drive acceptable outcomes from unacceptable situations.

Embrace the learnings

I recently read about an experiment that was conducted on children to establish how they would respond to failure. In this experiment, one at a time, the children were provided an easy puzzle to complete and then a really tough one. The expectation was that having easily completed the first they would show signs of how they dealt with failure when faced with the second. However, this was not the case. A number of the children rolled up their sleeves relishing the challenge and enjoying the task even though they did not manage to complete it. The reason was that they saw it not as a failure but as a learning experience where they would gain greater knowledge and skills to achieve it next time round.

The current thinking is that as we age and experience life and the pressures for success we tend to lose this mindset, or at least seldom use it for fear of failure. Through positive thinking, you should act more like the child and embrace failure as simply a means to learn to do it differently next time.

To help you here we should revert back to the results from the 'Explore' principle and use them in the Embrace Principle by forming powerful positive affirmations from your past experiences. These affirmations aren't just words; they are your battle cries against renewed adversity. For instance, if you've faced a setback at work, your affirmation might be, 'I embrace challenges as opportunities for growth', and 'I am resilient in the face of setbacks'. You can stand fully behind these affirmations because they have been taken from your true life's past experiences and not just made up for having something 'nice' to say to yourself. Use them to spur you on and search for a positive outcome.

By using the +Point Process you will become better equipped mentally and emotionally to face new setbacks even catching them before they transition from mere challenges. Remember that few things ever become true setbacks and by applying similar skills earlier in the process you can plot your course to avoid the storm clouds altogether.

Case Studies of Setback Resilience

To turbocharge your resilience-building journey, let's draw inspiration from real-life stories of individuals who faced immense setbacks and emerged stronger than ever. These case studies are not tales of unattainable heroism but real-life examples of people just like you and me who discovered their inner strength through positive thinking and perseverance.

Elon Musk:

Elon Musk, known as the visionary entrepreneur of our time, has displayed remarkable resilience throughout his career. His journey to revolutionize space travel and electric vehicles through SpaceX and Tesla has been riddled with challenges:

SpaceX Rocket Failures: Remember I previously mentioned that Musk's SpaceX company encountered several rocket failures during its early years. The first rocket that SpaceX developed, the Falcon 1, had catastrophic failures on each of their first three attempts. These failures nearly ruined the company and could have easily discouraged him from further attempts. However, Musk saw these failures as essential learning experiences, reframing them as opportunities to identify weaknesses and improve the technology that his team was working on. This process eventually led to the successful launch and landing of reusable rockets which has completely revolutionized space flight for mankind. This relentless pursuit of excellence and refusal to give up in the face of setbacks exemplifies his resilience.

Tesla's Financial Crises: Tesla, under Musk's leadership, faced severe financial crises. The electric car company was on the brink of bankruptcy at times. Despite all the odds, Musk continued to invest his time, energy, and personal fortune into Tesla. His unwavering belief in the electric vehicle industry and his determination to make it succeed not only saved Tesla but turned it into a major player in the automotive world prompting the global transition to electric automotive and the benefits related to it.

Musk's resilience isn't just about bouncing back from failures; it's about intentionally using setbacks as stepping stones toward his audacious goals. He leveraged adversity to fuel his motivation, ensuring that his vision for the future of space travel and sustainable transportation was successful.

Oprah Winfrey:

Oprah's journey from a troubled childhood to becoming a media mogul is a testament to her extraordinary resilience:

Discrimination and Personal Hardships: Growing up in poverty and facing discrimination as an African-American woman in the media industry, Oprah could have easily succumbed to adversity. However, she used her difficult upbringing as a source of strength, empathy, and motivation. Oprah's personal hardships and experiences informed her approach to connecting with audiences and addressing important societal issues on her talk show.

Professional Setbacks: Oprah experienced professional setbacks as well. Her early career included being fired from a television anchor spot. Instead of letting this setback define her, Oprah shifted her perspective. She viewed it as an opportunity to explore new avenues and eventually found her calling in talk show hosting.

Through her resilience, Oprah didn't just overcome obstacles; she transformed them into opportunities for personal growth and societal impact. Her journey serves to inspire us to embrace challenges as chances for both personal and professional development.

J.K. Rowling:

J.K. Rowling's path to literary success is a story of resilience, especially considering her early struggles:

Rejection from Publishers: Rowling faced rejection from numerous publishers when she was trying to get her first Harry Potter book published. Her manuscript was declined multiple times before finally Bloomsbury, a relatively small publishing house, took a chance on her. Rowling's resilience shone through her perseverance. She didn't let the setback of rejection deter her from pursuing her dream of sharing her magical world with readers.

Financial Hardships as a Single Mother: Rowling was a struggling single mother, grappling with financial difficulties while trying to write her book. Her determination to provide a better future for her child fueled her commitment to her writing. She often wrote in cafes while her baby daughter napped, showcasing her resilience in the face of adversity.

Rowling's resilience not only led to her literary success but also created a global phenomenon with the Harry Potter series. Her story teaches us that perseverance and determination can turn rejection and hardship into literary and cultural success.

Embracing Setbacks as Opportunities

Remember, setbacks are not the end of your journey; they are opportunities for growth and transformation. Yes, they will test

your resolve but by the same token, they will reveal your true potential. Armed with the power of positive thinking and the +Point
Process, you can now navigate life's challenges with unwavering
optimism.

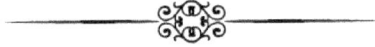

Chapter Twenty-Two

28 Days (Plus One) Later

"Staying positive in a negative world isn't naive; it's leadership." [1]

⚜

Congratulations, you've embarked on an incredible journey over the past 28 (+1) days, using The +Point Process to navigate challenges, build resilience, and embracing positive thinking to change your life.

Together we have climbed mountains, crossed turbulent seas, mined great depths, and discovered that the most exceptional destination is within ourselves. Today, we chart a course to make this voyage a never-ending adventure. Trust me, it's worth every moment of the journey.

---

1. Ralph Marston.(n.d.) As cited in James Jackson (2023) The +Point. The Power of Positive Thinking for Everyone!

Maintaining Positivity: A Journey Without End

You've unlocked the power of your mind and harnessed it to transform your life. But this journey is far from over. Now comes the thrilling part: sustaining this newfound outlook and making it a permanent companion on your life's expedition.

Reflect on Your Progress: A Positive Journal of Success

We have established that creating a positive mindset starts with self-awareness and likewise, maintaining positivity starts and continues with the need for self-awareness. You've spent the past four weeks exploring your inner landscape, creating powerful affirmations, and navigating challenges with unwavering optimism. Continue this journey by reflecting on your progress.

Continue your daily journaling exercises. Dedicate a few moments each day to jot down your thoughts, accomplishments, and areas where you've noticed a positive change. This habit will keep you grounded and serve as a compass for your continued growth and commitment.

The same is said for your gratitude diary. As you've discovered, gratitude is a potent force. Maintain a separate gratitude diary, where you write down things you're thankful for on a daily basis. This practice will keep your heart open and your spirit soaring high.

Embrace the Power of Routine: Your Daily Positive Rituals

Consistency is the key to lasting change. Develop daily rituals that reinforce your positive thinking:

Morning Affirmations:

Kickstart your day with a series of personalized affirmations, taken from your actual life experiences. These will remind you of your capabilities, strength, and purpose. They will highlight where you have tackled similar situations and been successful. They will be your constant supporters, reinforcing the knowledge and belief that you now hold the power of positive thinking to drive your success in good times and bad. Through your hard work and actual experiences, you have been instrumental in building up your resilience to negativity and will be able to overcome any challenge or setback with grace and determination.

Meditation and Mindfulness:

You are important and as such you need to maintain time for yourself. Dedicate this time to meditation and mindfulness exercises to stay connected with the present moment. Remember the breathing exercise. This may have seemed so irrelevant to begin with but hopefully, you have learned through the continued practice, that simply taking time out to concentrate on yourself to reach a place of calm within your being has been well worth it. Continue these practices to cultivate inner peace and ongoing resilience.

Cultivate a Positive Environment

Surround yourself with positivity. It can be a very negatively biased world out there so be selective with what and who you interact with. By being cognizant of the company that you keep you can start to remove negativity from your life. Think about social feeds, news, and other sources of negative influence and try to restrict these wherever possible. Spend time with people who uplift and inspire you. Remember positivity is contagious!

Declutter Your Physical Space:

It is really important to maintain a tidy, well-organized living and working environment around you. This will have a profound impact on your mindset. Clean and declutter your space regularly to maintain a sense of calm and clarity.

Continue Learning and Growing

The journey to lasting positivity is one of ongoing growth. Take to reading inspirational books to expand your horizons on personal development and positive thinking. Seek new insights to keep your journey fresh and exciting. This could also involve seeking out and attending workshops and seminars. These events can provide you with a renewed sense of purpose and connect you with like-minded individuals.

Share Your Journey

You're not alone on this path. There are literally millions of people out there that are in need of what you now possess. Share your knowledge and experiences with others. Not only does this reinforce your own understanding, but it also benefits those around you.

Expected Results: The Journey Continues

As you continue to utilize positive thinking in your everyday life you'll find that it becomes an integral part of your identity. Negativity loses its grip, and you will be better equipped to handle life's challenges and setbacks. You'll see the world through a brighter lens and inspire those around you with your resilience and optimism.

Remember, the journey doesn't have an endpoint; it's a lifelong adventure. Embrace it, nurture your positivity, and let it guide you through the ebbs and flows of life. The best part is that you're now in control of your destiny, and every day is a new opportunity to continue growing and flourishing.

So, my fellow traveler, the path to positivity stretches infinitely before you. Embrace it, enjoy it, and savor it every step of the way. Your transformed self will be your most exceptional and enduring accomplishment.

—————⊰✦⊱—————

Bringing others along on the journey

Positivity is contagious, and you now have the power to inspire those around you. Here's how you can bring others along on your journey:

Lead by Example:

Your transformed outlook on life will naturally influence those close to you. What initially may have seemed an interesting (possibly weird) change in your behavior will be seen by others over the longer term as a refreshing reawakening and one that drives your success. You can be the living proof of how positive thinking can create meaningful change both at home and at work which others can look up to.

Share Resources:

Recommend books, articles, or apps that have been instrumental in your journey. Encourage others to explore the +Point Process for themselves and start their own transformative process.

Support and Encourage:

Offer a listening ear and a supportive shoulder to those who express interest in positive thinking, or those who are suffering from negativity overload. Please share your experiences, challenges, and triumphs, and let them know that they are not alone on this path.

Organize Workshops:

Consider hosting workshops or group sessions to teach others about the +Point Process. These gatherings can provide a structured environment for learning and practicing positivity together. There's nothing more fulfilling than enabling and empowering others to gain the success they deserve through a positive thinking mindset.

Online Communities:

Join or create online communities dedicated to positive thinking and personal growth. These platforms can connect you with individuals who share your journey and provide a space for ongoing discussions.

Conclusion: Your Journey Continues

As you move forward remember that the +Point Process is not just a tool but a way of life. Positivity is a daily practice, a mindset, and a source of endless possibilities. By maintaining the habits and strategies that you've learned, you'll continue cultivating a life filled with purpose, resilience, and unwavering optimism.

Your transformation is an ongoing story, and each day is a new chapter waiting to be written. Share your successes, keep learning, and inspire others to join you on this incredible journey of personal growth and positivity. The world is brighter with your +Point mindset in it.

You've got this!

Chapter Twenty-Three

Jackson's Bonus Chapter

"People who are crazy enough to think they can change the world are the ones who do" [1]

Welcome to what I like to describe as the 'Bonus Chapter', or the underside of a Muller Yoghurt's foil lid. This is where I just can't end the book unless I have extended the topic onto a juicy subject of conversation. Today's juicy subject is **Motivation Powered by Positive Thinking**. You see positive thinking should not be viewed solely in its own right. It is more akin to a 100kwh Lithium-ion battery. Plug it into anything remotely aerodynamic and it will go like shit off a shovel. Positive thinking will fundamentally change your life, at home, at work, at everywhere. The ability to turn a negative into a positive, or at least less negative, is a life

1. Rob Siltanen, (1997), Apple's Think Different Campaign

skill that we are all born with but most of the human population loses through the trials and tribulations of simply living. To have it, nurture it, grow it, and use it on a daily basis is a privilege and will absolutely help power your success.

Motivation requires a positive mindset. It just does. Have you ever tried motivating someone who is utterly negative towards doing something? Oh my god, it's like pushing water uphill without getting your clothes wet. Now inversely, if you are able to motivate that person to view that 'something' as a positive that they want to do or achieve, then life gets a whole lot easier. But just like drinking five pints on an empty stomach, it's not something you should do unless you too are full of positivity and optimism, and you know where the bathroom is.

So what I'm saying here is that once you have a habit for positive thinking you can use its enormous power in a variety of ways in your life including powering the motivation of yourself and others around you. Let's explore how.

Motivation Powered by Positive Thinking

Are your positive thinking batteries all fully charged? Good. Then let's go.

You've already trekked through the wilderness of self-discovery, scaled the cliffs of positivity, and even camped under the starry skies of resilience and perseverance. But what's the secret sauce that gets us moving on this journey in the first place? Motivation, of course!

Motivation is actually a rather complex and multi-faceted beast, but it can be generally defined as the driving force that initiates, guides, and maintains goal-oriented behaviors. Motivation is what prompts individuals, you, me, and everyone to take action, pursue goals, and strive for achievement. It is the internal or external stimulus that influences and energizes us to act in a particular way, to work towards a goal, or to fulfill a specific need or desire.

You can be self-motivated based on a strong personal desire or internal need to do something, which is called intrinsic, or you can be motivated by someone or something externally possibly through rewards or pressure which is called extrinsic. It can also be influenced by various factors, including personal values, interests, social or environmental circumstances, and most importantly by your emotional state.

The Motivation Maze

You might now find yourself wondering, "Do I need motivation to think positively, or should I think positively to get motivated?" Well, in a classic chicken-and-egg conundrum, they actually fuel each other. Together let's crack the code and understand this dynamic dance between positive thinking and motivation.

Positive Thinking: The Spark

Picture this: It's morning, and you wake up thinking, "Today is going to be awesome!" Instantly, your brain does a happy dance and releases a cocktail of feel-good neurotransmitters, such as dopamine and serotonin. These little guys get to work and set the stage for a motivation boost, like your trusty partner who pushes you gently out of bed, ready to conquer the day ahead.

The Motivation Engine

So, your positive thoughts are like the high-powered battery pack that powers the motivation engine. Once your motivation is running, it's time to hit the accelerator and take action. Remember, it's not just about thinking positively; it's about channeling that positivity into action. Motivation is the bridge that takes you from contemplation to execution.

Stoking the Motivation Flame

Now that we've acknowledged the indispensable partnership between motivation and positive thinking, it's time to ignite the engines and hit the open road of action and purpose. You're about to embark on an adventure, and this journey will be nothing short of extraordinary.

Set the GPS (Goals Positioning System)

If motivation were a car, goals would be its guiding GPS. Imagine these goals as exciting destinations along your journey, awaiting your arrival. Your positive thoughts have already armed you with the belief in your abilities, so it's time to make these goals crystal clear. Think SMART: Specific, Measurable, Achievable, Relevant, and Time-bound when setting these goals.

Specific: means knowing exactly where you're going.

Measurable: ensures you can track your progress like your mileage on a road trip.

Achievable: ensures that you're setting yourself up for success rather than failure and frustration.

Relevant: means that your goals align with your journey, just as you choose destinations in sync with your route.

Time-bound: means you've set a clear timeframe for your goals, much like planning rest stops along the way.

This approach is like having your GPS set for your dreams, ensuring that you navigate your way to your most treasured destinations with precision and without wasting time in dive bars along the way.

Lights, Camera, Action!

Your positive thinking is the lens through which you perceive your success. Now, harness that power by crafting mental movies in high-definition. Visualize yourself, not as an onlooker, but as the protagonist, achieving your goals. See the finish line vividly, feel the exhilaration that comes with accomplishment, and let this mental reel drive your motivation to take action. It's the fuel that propels your dreams forward and makes them a tangible reality.

Positivity Squad

Consider the people around you as your adventure companions. These individuals play a significant role in influencing your positivity and motivation. Much like selecting your road trip companions, choose your companions wisely. You wouldn't want anyone to get car sick along the way. Instead surround yourself with those who radiate positivity, those whose motivation inspires and uplifts you. By sharing your journey with these people, you'll create a symphony of motivation that resonates through your every endeavor. Not only that but your well-chosen travelling companions will not only stick with you until your journeys end but will likely advise you of new places to visit.

The Chorus of Affirmations

Positive self-talk is more than just a confidence booster; it's your secret weapon for motivation. When your inner voice takes on the role of a personal cheerleader, you'll find yourself pumped up and ready to face challenges head-on. The pessimistic naysayers won't stand a chance against the powerful affirmations you create based on your true life's achievements. These personalized affirmations, crafted with positive thinking act as your cornerstone, bolster your motivation, fuel your determination, and propel you forward for success.

Dance with Small Wins

In this exhilarating journey towards motivation and success, every triumph, no matter how seemingly small, demands not just acknowledgment but also a spirited celebration. Think of it like cruising down a sun-soaked interstate, with your goals shimmering like magnificent stop-off points along the way. Now, each of these goals can be seen as your dreamy mini-destinations, with positive thinking acting as your trusty road map.

Each time you hit one of these stops, let it be a memorable experience. Visualize it as that fantastic roadside diner, there are some I promise you, offering up the most mouthwatering lunch you've ever tasted. As you dine on each victory, take a moment to savor the flavors of your accomplishment. Relish the sensations of progress, no matter how incremental they may seem.

Think of your small wins as the appetizers to your main meal. Each one leaves you craving for more. As you start to accumulate ever greater numbers of them, they become the appetizers of momentum, gradually building into a feast of motivation that keeps you moving forward.

So, crank up your favorite songs and dance through these small wins as they play out on your motivational soundtrack of life.

Introducing the Jackson Challenge: The Positive Thinking Dance-Off!

Yes, you heard that right!

Prepare for a challenge like no other, an electrifying dance-off with the most formidable opponent you'll ever face: yourself! This isn't your ordinary morning routine; it's a vivacious dance extravaganza designed to turbocharge your motivation and stoke the flames of positive thinking. No, I have not gone crazy!

So, what's the game plan? Each morning, select a happening beat that ignites your spirit and crank up the volume like you're about to set the dance floor on fire. The best part? You can dance like nobody's watching because, well, they're not.

As you lose yourself in the rhythm, focus your thoughts on your goals, your dreams, and your unstoppable potential to conquer the world. Let your moves mirror your inner positivity and motivation. Feel the groove and unleash your inner 'Just Dance' champion.

But here's the science behind the dance: it's an endorphin party! Yes, that's right—dancing floods your brain with endorphins, those delightful little chemicals that do their own dance inside your head to elevate your mood. Now, pair these endorphins with your positive thoughts, and you've got a motivational mix that's truly off the charts. You'll kickstart your day with a surge of inspiration like never before.

And guess what? You're not alone in this adventure. Capture your daily dance-off on video and share it with your positivity squad. They'll gladly jump in, and together, you'll ignite a positivity-infused dance revolution. Your groovy moves and positive vibes will inspire and motivate each other, creating a camaraderie that's as infectious as it is empowering.

So, turn up the music, let your feet set the pace, and dance your way to boundless motivation. This unique challenge will engrave the unbreakable link between positive thinking and motivation in your memory, as well as give you a little early morning cardio.

As you embrace this extraordinary challenge, get ready for an adventure like no other. The road ahead may be winding, but your unwavering companions—motivation and positivity—will light the way. Lace-up those dancing shoes because we're about to dance our way to an extraordinary destination! A brighter, more positive future!

Chapter Twenty-Four

Jackson's Awesome Extra Bit

"The moments of happiness we enjoy take us by surprise. It is not that we seize them, but that they seize us"[1]

Just when you thought it was all over...

Yep, I've got something more and very exciting for you all. I'm calling this **'Jackson's Awesome Extra Bit'** for no other reason than I think it sounds pretty cool. I have added some additional content that I have been mulling over for inclusion in a new book which you can get your hands on for free from my publisher's website, 3eyepublishing.com, under the resources section. Or if you are reading this on your funky digital device you can click

---

1. Ashley Montagu, (n.d.) As cited in James Jackson (2023) The +Point. The Power of Positive Thinking for Everyone!

'HERE' and read all about me (or skip that part) and go straight for the freebie section under resources. I certainly hope that you enjoy it and you can always leave a comment or at least your details so that my publisher can feel good that they have some subscribers and you will feel good because you will get to know when the next book finally launches. Win-win!

Book Reviews

Now this is where I need your help, or rather the other 8.0999 99999 residents on this amazing planet do. We need to get the word out there that there is a cure for all the negative thinking swilling about and that we have it here all neatly contained in one small friendly book. One way to do that is for each of you who have found this book enthralling, entertaining, and positively enlightening to go out and purchase ten further copies and give them to all those who desperately need our help. This will achieve several exciting outcomes; Firstly your friends and colleagues will forever be in your debt, secondly, they will be awestruck at your sudden and well-received generosity, and thirdly you will be ensuring that every time you meet them again in the future that your conversations will be a whole lot more positive than they were before. This approach I would highly recommend.

Another way is to simply pop over to Amazon and provide a great book review so that when other seekers of positivity come across The +Point in their search they will know that salvation is at hand and that you are all pointing them toward a world where negativity has been banished forever. Whilst this is not as great as option one it will certainly help your fellow humans.

With that, I will leave you with one final thought; ***"Just remember, your positivity is the most contagious thing you'll ever spread"***.

Thank you to Walmart, IKEA, and all the other unnamed retail enterprises that crafted my early years.

And to Becky from Starbucks – Now you know what to write on the side of the cup.

About the Author

"Life is like a rollercoaster. Try not to scream too much, and keep your arms and legs inside at all times."[1]

Jackson James

Jackson James, is a maverick wordsmith, a citizen of the world who's navigated more continents than most people do in a game of Risk. Hailing from the bustling labyrinth of London, UK, and educated at Cambridge, Jackson the eternal student has devoted several lifetime's efforts to the pursuit of knowledge, culminating in a masterful understanding of Psychology and Human Interaction. To keep things balanced he later added 'Positive Psychology' to his academic repertoire boosting his Scrabble word score by 37– *an act of sheer linguistic genius!*

---

1. (n.d.) As cited in James Jackson (2023) The +Point. The Power of Positive Thinking

His eclectic career reads like an anthology of genres, from retail to tech wizardry, to consulting across global conglomerates. While others may puzzle over the complexities of modern gadgetry, Jackson chose to venture into the even more intricate terrain of human behavior and psychology. Recently taking the ultimate plunge, diving headfirst into the mysteries of unconventional thinking, dissecting the enigmatic human psyche, and sharing his findings through his writings.

His work is a multi-dimensional mirror reflecting the intricate tapestry of the human experience. Within its threads, you'll find elements of self-discovery, personal growth, and visionary leadership. But this isn't just about the mind; it's also about embracing the heart, the spirit, and a relentless passion for life's most profound mysteries.

Today, Jackson wears several jaunty hats – writer, life coach, mentor – and he wears them with the infectious enthusiasm of a true trailblazer. His unapologetically upbeat and quirky style is a magnet for those who dare to question the norm and explore the boundaries of their potential.

So, dear reader, embark on this journey with Jackson James and brace yourself for an expedition of enlightenment, hilarity, and unapologetic enthusiasm. Whether you're a seasoned explorer of the human psyche or a newcomer to the world of positive thinking, Jackson is your fearless companion on this incredible adventure. Get ready to push the boundaries, unleash your inner maverick, and embrace the +Point of view for a lifetime of extraordinary experiences.